The Food Lover's Guide to
Meat and Potatoes

The Food Lover's Guide to

Meat and Potatoes

Sharon Tyler Herbst

William Morrow and Company, Inc.
New York

Library of Congress Cataloging-in-Publication Data

Herbst, Sharon Tyler.
    The food lover's guide to meat and potatoes / Sharon Tyler Herbst.
  —1st ed.
        p.   cm.
    Includes index.
    ISBN 0-688-13771-7
    1. Cookery (Meat)   2. Cookery (Potatoes)   I. Title.
TX749.H47   1996
641.6'6—dc20   95-46280
                                                      CIP

Printed in the United States of America

First Edition

1 2 3 4 5 6 7 8 9 10

BOOK DESIGN BY RICHARD ORIOLO

Acknowledgments

A basic truth known to every author is that that a book would simply not become a book without the intricate support system composed of family, friends and colleagues. And so, with tremendous gratitude and affection, I offer a heartfelt thank-you and verbal hug to…

Ron Herbst, my husband, hero and best friend, for being my business and creative consultant, spirit lifter, computer expert, trusted taster and, when there was little time for anything but writing and testing, for cooking dinner or taking me out.

Harriet Bell, my exceptional editor, who enthusiastically enlightens, guides and believes in me, and whose sense of humor *always* makes me laugh.

Gail Kinn and Ann Bramson, the wonderful editors who made sure this book received the perfect finishing touches.

Sonia Greenbaum, copy editor, who so skillfully minded my *p*'s and *q*'s and even found a better way to express some of my ideas.

All the behind-the-scenes people at Morrow, who so diligently worked on the design, layout, printing and everything else it took to bring this book together.

Fred Hill, my literary agent, for his insight, guidance and urbane wit.

Bob Tomlin, meat department manager at Petrini's market, for his ready smile and invaluable advice concerning all aspects of meat.

The dear friends who have been willing and enthusiastic tasters, sampling dishes both wonderful and not-so-wonderful-yet, making suggestions and generously sharing ideas:

Sally and Stan Bernstein, Bobbi and Ted Campagna, Ruth and Phil Hicks, Lee and Susan Janvrin, Glenn and Laura Miwa, and Dan and Kimberley Young.

And, as always, my dear parents, Kay and Wayne Tyler, and sister, Tia Tyler Leslie, for their unending encouragement, love and support (and their gentle exhortations not to work so hard).

Contents

Introduction

✦

Meat and Potatoes—
a Timeless Appeal

*At the end of a long, hard day, a young man's
fancy turns to meat and potatoes.*

It's true that few things set mouths to watering more than the time-honored combination of meat and potatoes—an alliance that, for many, is synonymous with comfort food. There's a feeling of old-fashioned virtues that accompanies meat and potatoes which—individually and in concert—have, for centuries, been supplying body and soul with satisfaction. Cooks and diners alike appreciate the simple pleasures of these two extraordinarily satisfying foods.

But that wasn't always so. Although meat has been a staple since prehistoric times, the potato took much longer to secure its place in gastronomical history. It was cultivated by the Incas thousands of years ago, but Europeans were not so readily accepting. Religious rhetoric decried the humble tuber as suspect because it isn't in the Bible. The potato was also reputed to be a sexual stimulant, which further fueled clerical denunciations. And the potato's reputation was additionally hindered by suspicions that, because it's a member of the sometimes poisonous nightshade family (as are tomato, eggplant and belladonna), it was most certainly deadly.

In the sixteenth century, Sir Walter Raleigh was instrumental in debunking the poisonous potato myth when he planted the tuber on some of his property in Ireland. A hundred years later, the canny Irish, knowing a good thing when they saw it, were growing prodigious amounts of potatoes. Today, hundreds of varieties of this popular vegetable are grown around the world. And why? Because superstitions aside, it's simply hard to miss with a potato.

For the greater part of this century, the potato was maligned as being starchy and fattening and therefore not a good choice for the weight conscious. Now we know nothing could be further from the truth. In fact, the unassuming potato is fat-free, cholesterol-free and literally packed with nutrition (see "Food for Thought," page 55). Whether it's because it's a neat little package of nutrition or simply that it's so exceptionally satisfying, the potato ranks fourth as the world's most significant crop (wheat, rice and corn taking the leads). Potatoes are the favorite vegetable of Americans, who so love this venerable tuber that their annual per-capita con-

sumption is 125 pounds—more than twice as much as the second favorite, the tomato (which, actually, is a fruit).

Meat, of course, has been a popular dietary foundation for eons. It still is, even in the nutritional light of modern times. But today's meat is different than that of yesteryear, with beef, pork and lamb all being bred leaner than before. The dual evils of fat and cholesterol have, for most, forever banished the days when a 16-ounce steak was considered a virility symbol. Today's average serving is much less, with nutritionists advising that the daily cooked-meat consumption be no more than 6 ounces—a figure at which just as many scoff as embrace. Most health professionals agree that meat—a nutrient-dense food—is good for us as long as we don't go hog-wild on it. The truth is that most people know it doesn't take a huge serving of meat to be satisfied. Which is probably why these days meat is often served as a component of a main dish rather than the entrée itself. That way everybody wins, and without missing out on the benefits of meat.

Something the consumer *is* missing out on in most markets these days is a friendly butcher ready and waiting to answer questions on everything from what cut to buy to how to cook it. And that can be a problem because, for many of us, the profusion of neatly prepackaged meat cuts in self-service cases is immensely confusing, not to mention intimidating. All you really need to know are a few simple basics like where the cut comes from on the animal, which tells you what to expect in terms of tenderness (*see* "Some General Tips on Buying Meat," page 6, and the "Retail Cuts" charts on pages 9, 10, 11 and 12) and how best to cook the cut you buy (*see* "The Key to Success Is in the Cooking," page 15). If you're among the confused or intimidated, I hope this book will help dispel your angst and assist you in making the right buying and cooking decisions for a particular cut and quality of meat.

Together or separately, meat and potatoes lend themselves to a seemingly endless variety of combinations and cooking methods, and the recipes in this book run the gamut in category and style. Dishes range from down home (Heaven-and-Earth Pork Pot Pie and Smoky Spiced Brisket and Apples) to uptown (Veal Niçoise and French Lamb Chops with Minted Onion Marmalade), from quick and simple (Rip-Roaring Rib Eyes) to slightly more time-consuming (Potato-Chive Focaccia), and from company favorites (Potato Lasagne) to simple family fare (Mashed Potato–Stuffed Peppers). There are soups (Creamy Blue-Potato Bisque and Spud Chili), sandwiches (Meatball Muffuletta and Herbed Potato Burgers) and even a salad (Sweet 'n' Sassy Potato-Sausage Salad) and dip (Skordalia). Some recipes take more time than others, but none are difficult. In the end, I trust that all the following recipes render rib-stickin', soul-nourishing goodness and satisfaction while at the same time delivering palate-pleasing pleasure.

Meat

The First Step: Buying Meat

The success of any dish depends on the food's quality, and that's particularly true of meat. You'll be ahead of the game if you know three things about the meat you buy: the *quality* (the grade of most meat sold to the consumer is Choice; Prime grade is generally reserved for restaurants and specialty butcher shops); *age* (the older the animal, the tougher the flesh); and *cut* (the part of the animal the meat comes from—that from the rib section, for example, is more tender than from the rump).

In many supermarkets these days it's not uncommon to see gleaming display cases brimming with glossy cellophane packages of shrink-wrapped meat and nary a butcher in sight. True, the labels contain most of the information you need: kind of meat (pork, beef, lamb); name of the wholesale cut (loin, shank); retail name of the cut (such as London broil); fat content (of ground meats); weight; price; and the date—usually the last date on which the meat should be sold. Still, it helps to know the basics. If your store has

How Much Meat Per Serving?

Meat is a nutrient-dense, complete protein, meaning it contains all the necessary amino acids. It also embodies a large amount of essential nutrients, including vitamin B_{12}, iron, niacin, phosphorus, protein, thiamine and zinc. Sounds like it's good for us, right? Well, it *is* but, as with most things, in moderation. Most nutritionists recommend servings of no more than 3 ounces of cooked meat (visualize a deck of playing cards), and advise no more than 2 servings a day. Three ounces of cooked meat are equal to about 4 ounces of raw, boneless, trimmed meat.

The amount of meat you buy per serving depends on the cut. Meat with a high proportion of fat and bone yields fewer servings than a boneless cut. For instance, bony meats, like spareribs, yield 1 to 2 servings per pound. Chops and bone-in steaks have a moderate amount of bone and therefore yield 2 to 3 servings per pound, whereas you can figure about 4 servings per pound for boneless roasts, ground meats, etc.

a service meat department, by all means ask questions. A butcher can make life immeasurably easier by showing you the basic differences in meat color, marbling, cuts, and so on; he or she can also tell you how to cook a particular cut. And you can save lots of time by having your butcher bone meat, cut it up for stew, cut pockets in roasts and thick chops, and so forth— services that are all free. Many markets and butcher shops don't customarily carry special cuts such as a crown pork roast or rack of veal, so be sure to order these cuts ahead of time.

Some General Tips on Buying Meat

• First of all, the process of freezing and thawing meat causes it to lose some of its natural juices, so always look for meat that hasn't been frozen.

• If the meat is prepackaged, make sure the wrapping is intact and tightly sealed to guard against deterioration and bacteria. Also, check the date code, which is usually the last date that meat should be sold but, in some stores, can refer to the date on which the meat was packaged (ask

Storing Meat

■ **Refrigeration:** Meat that will be cooked within 6 hours of purchase may be left in its shrink-wrapped packaging. Otherwise, remove the wrapping and rewrap loosely with waxed paper (so air can circulate around it); store in the coldest part of the refrigerator, such as the "meat compartment." Ground meats can be stored in this manner for 2 days; solid cuts up to 4 days.

■ **Freezing and defrosting:** Wrap meat airtight in vaporproof packaging (freezer bags, freezer wrap, heavy-duty foil, etc.), and freeze ground beef up to 3 months and solid cuts up to 6 months. When freezing ground-meat patties, steaks or chops, separate them with squares of plastic wrap—they'll be easier to pry apart for speedy defrosting. Defrost small cuts of frozen meat in the refrigerator overnight (longer for large cuts) or place the meat (still in its freezer-proof wrapping) in a large bowl of cool water—change the water every half hour until the meat is defrosted. Meat can be defrosted in a microwave oven (follow the manufacturer's instructions), but it should be cooked immediately thereafter since the microwave process actually can cook some portions of the meat.

■ **Storing and using leftovers:** Tightly cover and refrigerate leftover cooked meat up to 3 days. Before freezing leftover meat, plan how you will cook it and slice, dice or chop it accordingly. Measure the quantity (i.e., 1 cup) and label the package accordingly, including how it should be used (for stewing, sautéing, sandwiches, etc.). Leftovers can be used in salads, soups, stir-fries, dumplings, omelet fillings, stuffed peppers or acorn squash, meat loaf, pasta sauce, tacos or burritos. Or simply slice leftover meat for sandwiches, or, combine it with a sauce and serve over rice.

the butcher if this is unclear). Select packaged meat with an expiration date at least a day or two after the day you buy it.

• If you can visualize how an animal moves, knowing what parts are most tender becomes very logical. In general, the areas that are involved in locomotion or exercise—such as the rump and shoulder (from which come chuck, flank and shank cuts)—are more muscular and therefore leaner and tougher than the sections that are in the middle of the animal's body (for example, the loin and rib, from which come chops, steaks and roasts). The more inactive parts of the animal also have more marbling (flecks or streaks of fat running through them), which translates to juicier cooked meat. Lamb and veal are the exceptions to the rule because they're butchered young, before most parts have a chance to toughen, and therefore more of their flesh is tender.

• Bone-in cuts are almost always more flavorful than those that are boneless.

• In general, the darker the meat, the older the animal. Younger animals have more tender flesh.

• Bottom line: If cooked properly, *any* cut of meat can be delicious.

Buying Beef

• The United States Department of Agriculture (USDA) grades beef on three factors: (1) conformation (proportion of meat to bone), (2) finish (proportion of fat to lean), and (3) overall quality. The three top grades—Prime, Choice and Select—are those commonly available to consumers. Prime cuts are usually found only in upscale meat shops and fine restaurants. The meat's grade is stamped within a purple shield at regular intervals on the ouside of each carcass, so consumers rarely see the imprint. As with all of nature, the older the animal the tougher the meat.

• When buying beef, look for brightly colored, red to deep red cuts; marbling should be moderate. Avoid any meat with gray tinging or edges that look dry.

• The most tender beef cuts (rib, short loin and sirloin) come from the animal's most lightly exercised muscles, namely along the upper back. Heavily used muscles produce less tender cuts such as chuck (near the animal's front end) and round (from the rear).

• As a general rule, the less tender the cut, the cheaper it is and the longer it takes to cook. Moist-heat cooking methods (braising or stewing) are best for inexpensive cuts; tender cuts should be prepared with a dry-heat cooking method, such as broiling, frying or roasting.

Buying Lamb

• Lamb is meat from a sheep less than 1 year old. Baby lamb is slaughtered at 6 to 8 weeks; spring lamb is usually 3 to 5 months old. The younger the animal, the more tender it is. Animals slaughtered at 12 to 24 months are called yearlings; over 2 years old, they are considered mutton.

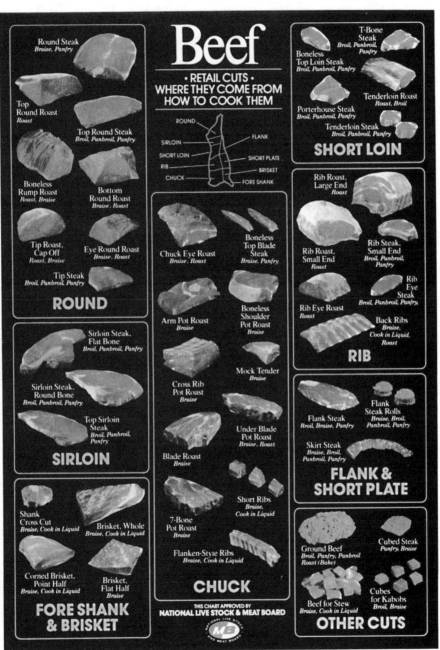

Beef

· RETAIL CUTS · WHERE THEY COME FROM HOW TO COOK THEM

ROUND

Round Steak
Braise, Panfry

Top Round Roast
Roast

Top Round Steak
Broil, Panbroil, Panfry

Boneless Rump Roast
Roast, Braise

Bottom Round Roast
Braise, Roast

Tip Roast, Cap Off
Roast, Braise

Eye Round Roast
Braise, Roast

Tip Steak
Broil, Panbroil, Panfry

SIRLOIN

Sirloin Steak, Flat Bone
Broil, Panbroil, Panfry

Sirloin Steak, Round Bone
Broil, Panbroil, Panfry

Top Sirloin Steak
Broil, Panbroil, Panfry

FORE SHANK & BRISKET

Shank Cross Cut
Braise, Cook in Liquid

Brisket, Whole
Braise, Cook in Liquid

Corned Brisket, Point Half
Braise, Cook in Liquid

Brisket, Flat Half
Braise

CHUCK

Chuck Eye Roast
Braise, Roast

Boneless Top Blade Steak
Braise, Panfry

Arm Pot Roast
Braise

Boneless Shoulder Pot Roast
Braise

Cross Rib Pot Roast
Braise

Mock Tender
Braise

Under Blade Pot Roast
Braise, Roast

Blade Roast
Braise

Short Ribs
Braise, Cook in Liquid

7-Bone Pot Roast
Braise

Flanken-Style Ribs
Braise, Cook in Liquid

THIS CHART APPROVED BY
NATIONAL LIVE STOCK & MEAT BOARD

SHORT LOIN

T-Bone Steak
Broil, Panbroil, Panfry

Boneless Top Loin Steak
Broil, Panbroil, Panfry

Tenderloin Roast
Roast, Broil

Porterhouse Steak
Broil, Panbroil, Panfry

Tenderloin Steak
Broil, Panbroil, Panfry

RIB

Rib Roast, Large End
Roast

Rib Roast, Small End
Roast

Rib Steak, Small End
Broil, Panbroil, Panfry

Rib Eye Steak
Broil, Panbroil, Panfry

Rib Eye Roast
Roast

Back Ribs
Braise, Cook in Liquid, Roast

FLANK & SHORT PLATE

Flank Steak
Broil, Braise, Panfry

Flank Steak Rolls
Braise, Broil, Panbroil, Panfry

Skirt Steak
Braise, Broil, Panbroil, Panfry

OTHER CUTS

Ground Beef
Broil, Panfry, Panbroil, Roast (Bake)

Cubed Steak
Panfry, Braise

Beef for Stew
Braise, Cook in Liquid

Cubes for Kabobs
Broil, Braise

Chart diagram labels: ROUND, SIRLOIN, SHORT LOIN, RIB, CHUCK, FLANK, SHORT PLATE, BRISKET, FORE SHANK

Meat

392500 06-406

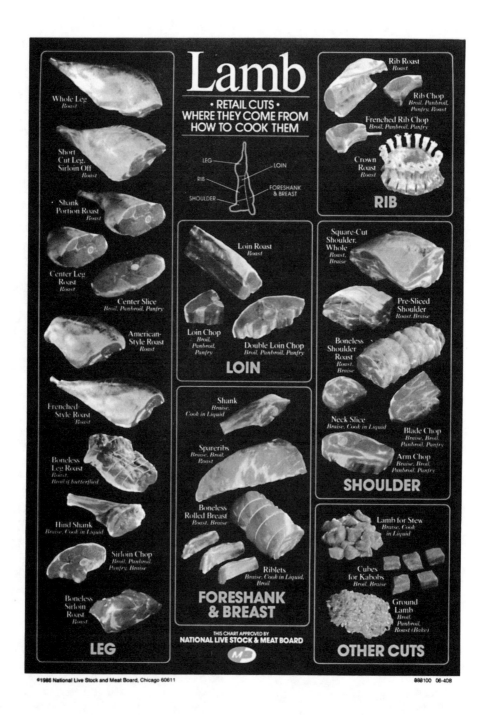

Lamb

• RETAIL CUTS •
WHERE THEY COME FROM
HOW TO COOK THEM

LEG — LOIN
RIB
FORESHANK & BREAST
SHOULDER

LEG

Whole Leg
Roast

Short Cut Leg, Sirloin Off
Roast

Shank Portion Roast
Roast

Center Leg Roast
Roast

Center Slice
Broil, Panbroil, Panfry

American-Style Roast
Roast

Frenched-Style Roast
Roast

Boneless Leg Roast
Roast, Broil if butterflied

Hind Shank
Braise, Cook in Liquid

Sirloin Chop
Broil, Panbroil, Panfry Braise

Boneless Sirloin Roast
Roast

LOIN

Loin Roast
Roast

Loin Chop
Broil, Panbroil, Panfry

Double Loin Chop
Broil, Panbroil, Panfry

FORESHANK & BREAST

Shank
Braise, Cook in Liquid

Spareribs
Braise, Broil, Roast

Boneless Rolled Breast
Roast, Braise

Riblets
Braise, Cook in Liquid, Broil

RIB

Rib Roast
Roast

Rib Chop
Broil, Panbroil, Panfry, Roast

Frenched Rib Chop
Broil, Panbroil, Panfry

Crown Roast
Roast

SHOULDER

Square-Cut Shoulder, Whole
Roast, Braise

Pre-Sliced Shoulder
Roast, Braise

Boneless Shoulder Roast
Roast, Braise

Neck Slice
Braise, Cook in Liquid

Blade Chop
Braise, Broil, Panbroil, Panfry

Arm Chop
Braise, Broil, Panbroil, Panfry

OTHER CUTS

Lamb for Stew
Braise, Cook in Liquid

Cubes for Kabobs
Broil, Braise

Ground Lamb
Broil, Panbroil, Roast (Bake)

THIS CHART APPROVED BY
NATIONAL LIVE STOCK & MEAT BOARD

©1986 National Live Stock and Meat Board, Chicago 60611

888100 06-408

Meat

10

• Color is the best guide for buying lamb—typically, the darker the color, the older the animal. Baby lamb is pale pink, regular lamb is pinkish-red. All lamb should have fine-grained flesh and creamy white fat.

• Choose a plump leg of lamb—the ratio of meat to bone and fat will be higher. The thin, parchmentlike coating (called "fell") on a leg of lamb retains the meat's juices, so don't remove it before cooking.

• Lamb chops fall into three categories: rib (the meatiest and most expensive), loin and shoulder (both less meaty, with a higher proportion of fat). Thick lamb chops (1 to 1½ inches) are more succulent after being cooked than thin ones.

• Remove most of the excess fat from lamb cuts to reduce the "lamby" flavor some people don't appreciate.

• The reason that most lamb (with the possible exception of older animals) tastes "lamby" to some is because it's overcooked. The flavor is rarely offputting if the lamb is cooked rare to medium.

• The strong flavor of older lamb can be diminished by rubbing a mixture of equal parts lemon juice and olive oil all over the meat's surface. Cover and refrigerate for 2 hours, then wipe dry and cook.

Buying Pork

• Choose fresh pork (meat other than bacon, ham and sausage) that has a pale pink color, a small amount of marbling and white (not yellow) fat. The darker pink the flesh, the older the animal.

• Trichinosis in pork is now rarely a problem, but one should never taste uncooked pork. Of course, take care to thoroughly

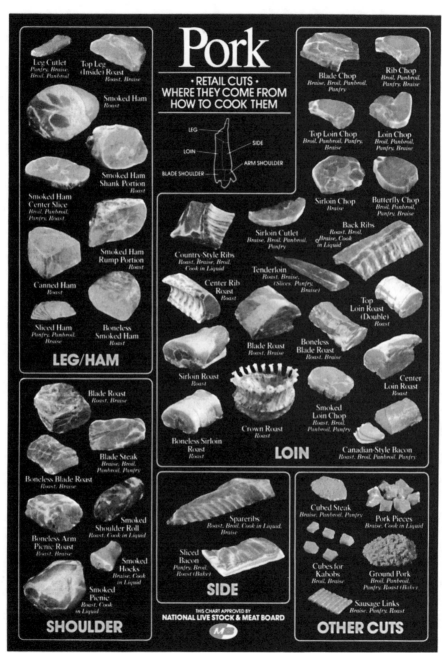

Pork

· RETAIL CUTS ·
WHERE THEY COME FROM
HOW TO COOK THEM

LEG
SIDE
LOIN
ARM SHOULDER
BLADE SHOULDER

LEG/HAM

Leg Cutlet
Panfry, Braise, Broil, Panbroil

Top Leg (Inside) Roast
Roast, Braise

Smoked Ham
Roast

Smoked Ham Shank Portion
Roast

Smoked Ham Center Slice
Broil, Panbroil, Panfry, Roast

Smoked Ham Rump Portion
Roast

Canned Ham
Roast

Sliced Ham
Panfry, Panbroil, Braise

Boneless Smoked Ham
Roast

SHOULDER

Blade Roast
Roast, Braise

Blade Steak
Braise, Broil, Panbroil, Panfry

Boneless Blade Roast
Roast, Braise

Smoked Shoulder Roll
Roast, Cook in Liquid

Boneless Arm Picnic Roast
Roast, Braise

Smoked Hocks
Braise, Cook in Liquid

Smoked Picnic
Roast, Cook in Liquid

LOIN

Blade Chop
Braise, Broil, Panbroil, Panfry

Rib Chop
Broil, Panbroil, Panfry, Braise

Top Loin Chop
Broil, Panbroil, Panfry, Braise

Loin Chop
Broil, Panbroil, Panfry, Braise

Sirloin Chop
Braise

Butterfly Chop
Broil, Panbroil, Panfry, Braise

Sirloin Cutlet
Braise, Broil, Panbroil, Panfry

Back Ribs
Roast, Broil, Braise, Cook in Liquid

Country-Style Ribs
Roast, Braise, Broil, Cook in Liquid

Tenderloin
Roast, Braise, (Slices: Panfry, Braise)

Center Rib Roast
Roast

Top Loin Roast (Double)
Roast

Blade Roast
Roast, Braise

Boneless Blade Roast
Roast, Braise

Sirloin Roast
Roast

Crown Roast
Roast

Center Loin Roast
Roast

Boneless Sirloin Roast
Roast

Smoked Loin Chop
Roast, Broil, Panbroil, Panfry

Canadian-Style Bacon
Roast, Broil, Panbroil, Panfry

SIDE

Spareribs
Roast, Broil, Cook in Liquid, Braise

Sliced Bacon
Panfry, Broil, Roast (Bake)

OTHER CUTS

Cubed Steak
Braise, Panbroil, Panfry

Pork Pieces
Braise, Cook in Liquid

Cubes for Kabobs
Broil, Braise

Ground Pork
Broil, Panbroil, Panfry, Roast (Bake)

Sausage Links
Braise, Panfry, Roast

1087150 06-407

Meat

wash in hot, soapy water anything (hands, knives, cutting boards, etc.) that comes in contact with raw pork.

• Cooking pork to an internal temperature of 137°F will kill any trichinae. However, to allow for a safety margin for thermometer inaccuracy, most experts recommend an internal temperature of 150° to 165°F. This range produces pork that's juicy and tender, whereas the 170° to 185°F range recommended in many cookbooks produces dry, over-cooked meat.

• For stuffed pork chops, choose loin or rib chops that are about 1½ inches thick. Have your butcher cut some for you if those displayed aren't thick enough; the butcher can also make a pocket for stuffing.

Buying Veal

• Though there are no precise age standards for veal, the term is generally used to describe a young calf 1 to 3 months old. However, many markets label as "veal" any meat that comes from animals up to 9 months old when slaughtered. Milk-fed veal is considered premium, and comes from calves that have been raised on milk. Their delicate flesh is firm and creamy white with a pale grayish-pink tinge. Other calves are fed grain or grass, which results in a slightly coarser texture and stronger flavor—the flesh is a pale pink color. Again, in general, the darker the meat, the older the calf.

• Choose fine-textured veal with a color varying from ivory with a pink tinge to creamy pink; the fat should be very white.

• Veal is so lean and delicate that it must be cooked very gently—more like poultry than beef. Moist-cooking methods like braising work well with veal, as do low-temperature roasting and brief sautéing.

• To keep it moist, a veal roast needs barding (covering with a layer of fat, which your butcher can do for you). Or you can lay strips of salt pork over the roast's surface. Likewise, ground veal needs added fat or it becomes too dry during cooking.

The nearer the bone the sweeter the meat.

—old English proverb

Meat

Veal

• RETAIL CUTS •
WHERE THEY COME FROM
HOW TO COOK THEM

LEG (ROUND)
SIRLOIN
LOIN
RIB
SHOULDER
FORESHANK & BREAST

Rib Roast
Roast

Boneless Rib Roast
Roast

Crown Roast
Roast

Boneless Rib Chop
Braise, Pantry, Broil

Rib Chop
Braise, Pantry, Broil

Short Ribs
Braise, Cook in Liquid

RIB

Blade Roast
Braise, Roast

Arm Roast
Braise, Roast

Blade Steak
Braise, Pantry

Arm Steak
Braise, Pantry

Boneless Shoulder Arm Roast
Braise, Roast

Boneless Shoulder Eye Roast
Braise, Roast

SHOULDER

Boneless Rump Roast
Braise, Roast

Round Steak
Braise, Pantry

Top Round Steak
Braise, Pantry

Leg Cutlet
Braise, Pantry, Broil

LEG (ROUND)

Breast
Braise, Roast

Boneless Breast Roast
Braise, Roast

Cross Cut Shank
Braise, Cook in Liquid

Riblet
Braise, Cook in Liquid

Shank
Braise, Cook in Liquid

FORESHANK & BREAST

THIS CHART APPROVED BY
NATIONAL LIVE STOCK & MEAT BOARD

Loin Roast
Roast

Boneless Loin Roast
Roast

Loin Chop
Braise, Pantry, Broil

Kidney Chop
Braise, Pantry

Top Loin Chop
Braise, Pantry, Broil

Butterfly Chop
Braise, Pantry, Broil

LOIN

Sirloin Roast
Roast

Boneless Sirloin Roast
Roast

Sirloin Steak
Braise, Pantry, Broil

Top Sirloin Steak
Braise, Pantry, Broil

SIRLOIN

Veal for Stew
Braise, Cook in Liquid

Ground Veal
Pantry, Broil

Cubes for Kabobs
Braise

Cubed Steak
Braise, Pantry

OTHER CUTS

The Key to Success Is in the Cooking

Cooking meat properly is the goal for any cook. The final result should be irresistibly tender and succulent. To begin with, here's a basic rule of thumb—tender meat cuts stay that way with brief dry-heat cooking methods like sautéing or broiling; less tender cuts benefit from lengthy, moist-heat techniques like braising or stewing. Of course, there are always exceptions to the rule: A well-marinated, scored flank steak (a fibrous, less-than-tender cut) is most delectable when grilled or broiled just a few minutes per side. Following are some salient points on the methods most commonly used to cook meat, preceded by some general tips for cooking meat.

General Tips on Cooking Meat

• If possible, remove meat from the refrigerator 30 to 60 minutes before cooking. Room-temperature meat browns faster and more evenly, and absorbs less fat than cold meat, which also tends to stick to the pan more than room-temperature meat.

• Trim all excess fat from meat. This not only reduces calories, but diminishes the risk of flare-ups during broiling and grilling.

• Slash the fat at ½-inch intervals along the edges of cuts like lamb and pork chops to keep them from curling during cooking.

• For the best browning, make sure the meat's surface is thoroughly dry. This is particularly important if the meat has been marinated. Paper towels make excellent blotters.

• Use a nonstick pan to reduce the amount of oil needed for browning meat.

• Unless the cut is very lean, it's often unnecessary to add fat or oil to aid in browning meat. Simply brush the bottom of the pan lightly with oil.

A Guide to Meat Temperatures

Type of Meat	Rare	Medium	Well-done
Beef	120°-135° F	140°-150° F	155°-165° F
Lamb	125°-140° F	145°-150° F	155°-165° F
Pork		150°-160° F	160°-170° F
Veal		140°-150° F	155°-165° F
Ham, cooked		130°-140° F	

Cutting Board Wisdom

■ The conventional wisdom for years has been that plastic cutting boards are better than their wooden counterparts for protection against food-poisoning bacteria. But just the opposite is true, say two microbiologists at the University of Wisconsin's Food Research Institute. Complex tests have proved that wooden cutting boards are actually so inhospitable to contaminants like meat and poultry juices that bacteria disappeared from wood surfaces within minutes. On the other hand, bacteria on the plastic boards multiplied at room temperature.

■ If you use plastic cutting boards, it's wise to have two—one for foods that will be eaten raw (such as salad ingredients) and one for foods that will be well cooked. Know that bacteria can accumulate in the knife cuts on plastic cutting boards—if your board is very scarred, buy a new one.

■ After each use, all cutting boards should be scrubbed thoroughly with hot water and detergent. Most plastic cutting boards can be washed in the dishwasher.

■ *Keeping cutting boards odor-free and clean:* Deodorize wood or plastic cutting boards by rubbing them with a paste of baking soda and water. Diminish discolorations by rubbing with lemon juice; let stand for 5 minutes before washing off. Sanitize boards by scrubbing them with a mixture of 1 quart hot water mixed with $1/3$ cup household bleach. Wash well with hot, soapy water.

• The temperature of the pan and any oil or fat in it should be very hot (but not smoking) before adding the meat.

• Dust the meat lightly with flour or cornstarch to facilitate browning when cooking in a little oil.

• Salt impedes browning and leaches some of the meat juices, so salt toward the end of the cooking time or after the meat is cooked.

• When browning meat, add 1 to 3 teaspoons of granulated sugar to the fat; heat, stirring often until the fat is hot, then brown the meat in it. The sugar caramelizes and gives the meat a beautiful color and delicious flavor.

- Remove excess fat from a pan with a baster.

- Because the juices in meat shift toward the center during cooking, the exterior becomes dry. Letting the meat "rest" for 10 minutes after it's finished cooking allows the juices to become redistributed throughout the meat and to set. This produces an evenly moist texture and makes the meat easier to carve. Keep the meat warm during this rest period by covering it lightly with foil.

Braising is a moist-heat cooking method used for less tender meat cuts. The meat is browned in a small amount of fat, then covered tightly and cooked in a small amount of liquid at low heat for a lengthy period of time. Braising may be done on the stovetop or in the oven. Almost any tough cut (brisket, short ribs, rump or shoulder roast, lamb or veal shanks, etc.) is well served with braising.

- Choose a heavy pot that's just slightly larger than the meat and liquid surrounding it. That way the meat, rather than the airspace, absorbs the heat. Brown the meat well before beginning to braise. First, blot off excess moisture from the meat's surface with a paper towel, then dredge the meat with flour or cornstarch. Be sure the fat is hot (not smoking) before adding the meat to be browned. Once browning is complete, pour off excess fat.

- Use only a small amount of liquid—too much, and the meat will poach instead of braise. Covering the meat with liquid transforms the cooking method into stewing.

- Instead of braising meat in water, try using more flavorful liquids like wine, beer, stock or vegetable juice.

- Tightly cover the pot as soon as the liquid has been added. If the pot cover doesn't fit securely, cover the pot with a piece of aluminum foil, then top with the lid.

- *For stovetop braising:* Reduce the heat to low or medium low, so the liquid is barely simmering.

- *For oven braising:* Cook in a preheated 300° to 325°F oven. Oven braising cooks meat more evenly because the heat surrounds the pot rather than coming only from the bottom.

- One of the big pluses of braised meat is that it can (indeed, some say *should*) be prepared a day or two before serving, for the flavors deepen and expand.

Broiling is a dry-heat method of cooking meat directly under the heat source. This method's good for ground meats and ten-

The Tender Touch

Most tough cuts (such as brisket, chuck or flank) benefit from tenderizing—pounding with a mallet, commercial meat tenderizer, marinating or moist-heat cooking methods.

■ Pounding meat tenderizes it by breaking down the tough fibers. Meat tenderizers made of metal and wood come in a wide variety of sizes, shapes and textures, and are found in kitchenware shops. Some have smooth surfaces while others are ridged.

■ Commercial meat tenderizers are typically in the form of white crystallized powder made from a papaya extract called "papain," an enzyme that breaks down tough meat fibers. South American cooks have been using papaya juice to tenderize meat for ages. Powdered meat tenderizer is available at most supermarkets. Most brands contain salt, sugar and calcium stearate, an anticaking agent. If possible, avoid tenderizers containing MSG (monosodium glutamate) or salt, both of which can extract some of the meat's natural juices. Homemade tenderizer can be made by pureeing a peeled and seeded papaya and rubbing it all over the meat's surface (or soak meat in canned papaya juice); cover and refrigerate for at least 3 hours. Scrape off papaya puree or pour off the juice; pat the meat dry with a paper towel before cooking.

■ Tea can also be used as a meat tenderizer, particularly for stew meat. In a Dutch oven, sear chunks of stew meat in fat or oil until very well browned. Add 2 cups strongly brewed black tea, bring to a boil, then cover and simmer for 30 minutes. Add stock and any other ingredients you wish, and continue cooking the stew as usual.

■ Soaking meat in a marinade (the softening ingredient is acid—vinegar, tomato juice, lemon juice, etc.)—for several hours to overnight also helps tenderize meat. The interaction of acids with some metals can transfer an unpleasant flavor to food, however, so marinate meat in a glass, enamel or other nonreactive container. Scoring the meat at $1/2$-inch intervals will help the marinade penetrate the flesh. Marinating is most successful when done in conjunction with another method like pounding or moist-heat cooking.

■ Moist-heat cooking (see BRAISING and STEWING) for a long period of time is probably the best way to tenderize a tough cut.

der cuts like rib and loin steaks and chops, but not appropriate for very lean meats like veal.

- Preheat the broiler and broiling pan.

- Before beginning to broil, blot off excess moisture from the meat's surface with a paper towel.

- Reduce the risk of flare-ups by trimming off excess fat.

- A recipe that says "broil 4 inches from the heat source" is referring to the measurement from the surface of the meat, not the bottom of the pan or rack on which the meat sits. Measuring the distance from the rack or pan positions the meat too close to the heat, which means it could burn before being properly cooked.

- A general rule of thumb: The thinner the meat, the closer to the heat source it should be. Rare-cooked steaks and other cuts should also be close to the heat. Thick cuts or those that are to be cooked well done should be positioned farther from the heat source.

- Drain off fat as it accumulates during broiling to help prevent fire.

- Smother a broiler fire by covering the pan with a large pan lid or sheet of heavy-duty foil.

- If the meat requires basting during broiling, warm the basting liquid first so it doesn't slow down the cooking process. Use only enough liquid to moisten the meat—too much will create steam, and the steak won't have the crisp surface usually created by broiling.

Grilling (also called *charcoal broiling*) is a technique by which meat is cooked outdoors over a heat source such as charcoal briquettes, gas, etc. Almost any meat can be grilled—tender cuts can be quickly grilled over medium heat while those less tender (like brisket) are best grilled over low heat for several hours.

- Never use a charcoal grill indoors or near dry areas that might catch fire.

- For faster-igniting charcoal, store it in airtight bags (like a large plastic trash bag) to keep it from absorbing moisture.

- Never add charcoal-lighting fluid to a fire that's already lit. And never use alcohol, gasoline or kerosene to start a charcoal fire.

- Charcoal briquettes are ready for cooking when they have a dull red glow and the surface is covered lightly by a gray ash.

- To test the heat level of a charcoal fire, place your palm at the cooking level. If you can keep it there for 2 seconds, the coals are HOT; 3 seconds, MEDIUM HOT; 4 seconds, MEDIUM; 5 seconds, MEDIUM LOW; and after 5 seconds the heat is considered LOW.

- For easier cleanup, coat the grill with nonstick vegetable spray before beginning to cook. Spray the grill away from the heat source so the oil won't cause a flare-up.

- For a smoky nuance, sprinkle coals with water-soaked wood chips (see page 81) just before beginning to grill.

- Flare-ups can be diminished by trimming excess fat from meat or by using lean ground meat. Or place a drip pan (any shallow pan without a handle) immediately beneath meat, stacking the coals on either side of the pan.

- Short on time? Give meats a jump-start by partially cooking them in the microwave oven and finishing up on the grill.

- Grilling will be more even if there's at least a 3/4-inch space between pieces.

- Most meats should be cooked over a medium fire—high heat is very drying.

- Thick foods like roasts require a slower fire to keep the exterior from burning.

- Always heat basting sauces—cold sauces slow down the cooking.

- Baste long-cooking meats only during the last 30 minutes of grilling, basting every 10 minutes for a multilayered glaze. If the sauce has a high sugar content (from molasses or tomato sauce, for example), which has a tendency to burn, don't start basting until the last 15 to 20 minutes.

- During the last 15 minutes of cooking time, don't baste with a marinade that hasn't been boiled. The cooking time may be too short to kill any bacteria that are transferred from the raw meat to the marinade.

- Remove meat from the grill a minute or two before it's done—heat conduction will continue to cook it.

Microwave cooking works by converting electric energy into microwave energy—short, high-frequency electromagnetic waves similar to those emitted by ordinary daylight and radio waves. This energy makes food molecules vibrate at an incredibly fast rate, creating the friction that heats and cooks the food. Microwaves, which are attracted to fat, moisture and sugar, cook from all directions (top, bottom and sides) at once and from the outside in, penetrating to a depth of only 1½ to 2 inches. The center of the food is generally cooked by heat conduction. Cooking times can vary immensely from oven to oven, so it's vital that you read the manufacturer's instruction booklet for your particular model and know your oven's wattage. If a recipe has been tested using a 700-watt oven, and yours is a 500-watt oven, you will definitely need to adjust the timing.

• Many characteristics affect how a microwave oven cooks meat: fat and/or bone distribution (microwaves are attracted to fat and will cook fatty meats more quickly); density (ground meat cooks faster than solid cuts); starting temperature (cold meat cooks slower than room-temperature meat); and shape—thin or small pieces cook faster than those that are thick or large.

• Microwave timing also depends on the volume of the meat being cooked. Two pork chops can take almost twice as long to cook as one.

• Cook tender cuts on HIGH (*100 percent power*); tougher cuts should be cooked with liquid at MEDIUM (*50 percent power*).

• "Braise" a roast in its own juices inside an oven-cooking bag (sealed with dental floss).

• Meat cooked in a liquid (like a stew) takes almost as long to cook in a microwave oven as it does on a stovetop.

• The temperature probe that comes with most microwave ovens can be an invaluable tool for cooking meats. Insert it deep in the meat so that it doesn't touch bone or fat.

• Because microwaves cook food at the outer edge of a plate first, arrange meat pieces (like chops) in a ring around the edge of the plate, the thickest or densest part of the meat pointing outward.

• Use the tines of a fork to pierce any meat enclosed in a membrane (like sausage) to prevent pressure from building up and exploding and making a terrible mess of your microwave oven.

• Browning meat on the stovetop before microwaving it will improve its final flavor and appearance. Or use a special microwave browning dish, which has a special coating that sears meat.

• If your microwave oven doesn't have a turntable, rotate meat a half-turn halfway through the cooking time to allow for hot spots.

• Allow for oven-wattage variances by checking meat for doneness at the minimum cooking time given in a recipe.

Testing Doneness with Meat Thermometers and Other Methods

■ **_Meat thermometers_** are invaluable kitchen tools. Using one means you'll no longer have to cut into meat (thus releasing some of its juices) to determine its doneness. There are two basic types of meat thermometers—regular and instant-read. A regular meat thermometer can be inserted in the meat at the beginning of the cooking time and left in throughout the duration. Instant-read thermometers are inserted in the meat toward the end of the cooking time and record the temperature in about 10 seconds. When buying a thermometer, choose one with a thin probe—it makes smaller holes from which the meat's juices can escape. It should have an easy-to-read scale indicating temperatures for each type of meat (beef, lamb, pork, etc.). It should be noted, however, that many meat thermometers suggest _very_ high temperatures which, if used as guidelines, would produce dry, overcooked meat. For an accurate reading, insert the probe so at least half of it is inside the meat. It should be positioned in the meat's thickest portion—if you hit bone, gristle or fat, the reading will be distorted.

To check a thermometer's accuracy, place it in boiling water for 3 minutes, at which time it should read 212°F. If it doesn't (say, it reads 202°F), adjust your recipe temperature accordingly (in this case, by 10 degrees). Therefore, if a recipe calls for an inner temperature of 160°F, cook the food to 170°F on your thermometer. (_Note:_ Water's boiling temperature at high altitudes is about 2 degrees lower per 1,000 feet above sea level.)

■ **_The touch technique:_** Though it takes practice, you can tell how a steak or chop is done by touch. Simply press the meat lightly with your finger: If it's soft, it's rare; if it resists slightly but springs back, it's medium rare; if the meat's quite firm, it's well done. A little practice makes perfect.

■ **_The skewer test:_** If you don't have either a meat thermometer or a knack for the touch technique, do this: Insert a metal skewer at the thickest point of the meat, leave it for 30 seconds, then remove and hold it against your bottom lip. A tepid skewer means the meat is rare, medium warm means it's medium and hot (be careful!) tells you that it's well done.

• As with conventional methods, food continues to cook after it's removed from the oven, so cook the meat to about 10°F less than the desired final temperature.

• Any meat benefits from being allowed to stand 5 to 15 minutes (depending on the size of the cut) to allow the juices to redistribute throughout the flesh.

Panbroiling is a dry-heat technique by which food is cooked in a heavy, ungreased skillet over moderately high to high heat. Like broiling, this method is good for ground meats and tender cuts like rib and loin steaks and chops, but not for lean meats like veal.

• For the best browning, blot the meat's surface dry with a paper towel.

• Never cover panbroiled meat—this will create steam and hinder a crusty surface.

• Any rendered fat should be poured off as it accumulates.

• Flip the meat often so it browns evenly.

Roasting is a method by which food is oven-cooked, uncovered, until the exterior is well browned and the interior tender and juicy. The best cuts for roasting are those that are both tender and large (the latter so they'll remain tender and moist).

• For this cooking method, a roast or other cut should be relatively large.

• Although boneless roasts may provide carving convenience, bones give meat a big flavor bonus.

• Bone-in cuts don't take as long to cook as those that are boneless—the bone acts as a heat conductor to the meat's center.

• Remove a large roast from the refrigerator 2 to 3 hours before cooking.

• Fat insulates the meat, adding moisture and flavor. Always cook a roast (or other cut) fat side up so the fat bastes the meat naturally as it melts.

• Cover the top of lean roasts with a layer of fatback or lightly salted bacon, a technique called barding. Or ask your butcher for thin pieces of fat to lay on top of the meat and naturally baste it.

• Rubbing exposed meat with vegetable oil helps retain the meat's natural moisture.

• For added flavor and color, sear meat in 1 to 2 tablespoons of hot oil over medium-high heat until nicely browned.

• Lightly dust meat with granulated sugar before roasting to give the surface the delicious flavor and dark brown color that come from the sugar's caramelization.

• Elevate meat on a roasting rack so the heat and air can circulate underneath, thereby cooking it more evenly.

• Always start roasting meat in a thoroughly preheated oven.

• Roasting meat at a low temperature for a relatively long time will result in a uniform internal temperature (medium, medium rare, etc.). The disadvantage is that the exterior of a slow-cooked roast is not well browned. Slow-cooked roasts shrink less than those cooked at higher temperatures.

• Roasting meat at a high temperature for a relatively short time creates a beautifully browned crust and a more succulent, flavorful flesh. Also, the finished roast will have a range of temperatures from well done to medium rare or rare. The disadvantage with high-temperature roasting is that there will be increased shrinkage.

• For the best of all possible worlds, start roasting meat at high heat, then reduce the temperature after 20 minutes.

• Turning meat at least twice during roasting helps to brown it evenly.

Sautéing (also called *panfrying*) cooks food in a small amount of fat over moderate to high heat. This cooking method is recommended for ground meat and tender cuts like rib and loin steaks and chops.

• Use a skillet or sauté pan with a handle and low sides; high pan sides can steam the meat before it's even sautéed.

• Thoroughly heat the oil before adding the meat to the pan.

• Blot the meat to be sautéed with a paper towel so it's as dry as possible.

• Sprinkling the meat with a little sugar before sautéing will produce a brown, caramelized (but not sweet) surface.

• If you have a large amount of meat to sauté, use two pans—the meat will brown better, cook more evenly and won't have a tendency to steam as it would if crowded in one pan.

• While the meat is sautéing, grab the handle and shake the pan often so the meat is tossed around and becomes evenly browned.

• Use a bulb baster to remove any excess grease (from rendered fat) from the pan.

• Never cover meat while it's sautéing or steam will gather and the meat will have a "damp" instead of crisp surface.

Stewing is almost identical to braising except that the meat is completely covered with liquid before being slowly simmered. The meat may be cut into small pieces or stewed whole, either on the stovetop or in the oven. Browning the meat before stewing is optional. Almost any tough cut (like brisket or lamb or veal shanks) is well served with stewing. *See* BRAISING for cooking tips.

Stir-frying consists of quickly frying small pieces or strips of food in a minuscule amount of oil over very high heat while constantly and briskly stirring. Small, tender pieces of meat are best for stir-frying.

• A wok is traditional for stir-frying, although any large, deep skillet will do. Stir-frying is a technique that needs plenty of room for ingredients to be tossed and stirred.

• When buying a wok, consider the following: Flat-bottomed woks are best for electric ranges, while gas ranges can accommodate either flat- or round-bottom models. When using a round-bottom wok, place the ring stand, narrow side up, over a large burner. There are also free-standing electric woks.

• Before starting to cook, heat the oil until a piece of vegetable sizzles when tossed into the pan.

• Reduce calories by spraying the room-temperature pan with nonstick vegetable spray. Heat the pan and cook the vegetables; add a tiny amount of oil when ready to cook the meat.

• Cook large amounts of meat in two batches. Otherwise, the pan will cool down too much and the meat will end up braising in its own juices rather than frying. Cook each batch until *almost* done to your liking, then transfer it to a plate and cook the second batch.

Hotline

Can't get an answer from your butcher or can't find one to talk to? Call the USDA Meat and Poultry Hotline at 1-800-535-4555, Monday through Friday, from 10 A.M. to 4 P.M., eastern time. In the Washington, D.C., area, call 202-447-3333.

Smoky Spiced Brisket and Apples

Brisket is the cut most commonly used to make corned beef. It's also the meat of choice for quintessential barbecue. There are two cuts of brisket: the *point cut* is the thicker of the two and is marbled with fat, which adds flavor; the *flat cut* is flat, thin and quite lean. Either cut will work for this recipe. This preparation method delivers the best of two worlds by combining the rich, smoky flavor of grilled brisket with the ease of oven braising. The purpose of the brief grilling is to smoke and brown the meat, not to *cook* it, so it's important for the vents to be barely open to keep the smoke in and the fire relatively low.

Although the garlic is cooked unpeeled, be sure to rub off any excess papery skin before putting it into the pot. Pop the buttery-soft cloves of cooked garlic out of their skins and spread either on the meat or chunks of hearty bread. Not only is leftover brisket great for sandwiches and cold beef salad, but it makes a remarkable hash.

Serves 6 to 8

2 teaspoons salt

1 1/2 teaspoons freshly ground black pepper

1 1/2 teaspoons ground allspice

1 1/2 teaspoons ground nutmeg, preferably freshly ground

3/4 teaspoon ground cinnamon

3/4 teaspoon ground cloves

3 tablespoons olive oil

4–4 1/2 pounds beef brisket, well trimmed of fat

2 medium onions, cut into 1/4-inch slices and separated into rings

3 cups beef broth

1 cup full-bodied red wine, such as Zinfandel or Cabernet Sauvignon

2 heads garlic, separated into cloves but unpeeled

4 medium-tart apples, cored and cut into eighths

The night (or at least 8 hours) before cooking the brisket, combine salt, pepper, allspice, nutmeg, cinnamon, cloves and 2 tablespoons of the oil in a small bowl; stir to make a paste. Rub paste over all surfaces of brisket, pressing into meat (if you don't want to use your fingers, use the back of a tablespoon). Wrap in plastic wrap and refrigerate.

At least 1 hour before grilling the brisket, soak 2 cups wood chips in water to cover; remove meat from refrigerator. Light fire in outdoor grill according to manufacturer's directions. Just before beginning to grill, sprinkle drained wood chips over heat source; adjust upper and lower grill vents so they're only open a quarter of the way. Place brisket on grill, making sure that spice rub stay on meat and not on plastic wrap. Cover grill and cook brisket for 10 minutes; turn meat and grill other side for 10 minutes.

Meanwhile, preheat oven to 350°F. Heat remaining 1 tablespoon oil in a Dutch oven or very large ovenproof pot. Over medium-high heat, sauté onions, stirring occasionally, until nicely browned, about 15 minutes. Add beef broth and wine; bring to a boil. Remove from heat; place smoked brisket on top of onions. Cover and bake for 1 hour. Add garlic; cover and bake 45 minutes, or until meat is fork-tender. Add apples; bake 10 more minutes.

Turn off oven. Transfer brisket, apples and garlic to a platter; return platter to oven with door open. Set the pot over high heat; cook until liquid is reduced by a third. Salt and pepper to taste. Slice brisket at an angle and across the grain. Pass the *jus* with the meat.

I have known many meat eaters to be far
more nonviolent than vegetarians.

—Gandhi

Ginger-Peanut Satay

Satays (pronounced sah-TAYS, and also spelled satés) are an Indonesian specialty found everywhere in their native country from street vendors to the finest restaurants. Delicious as appetizers, snacks or even as main courses, satays can be prepared well in advance. Whether made with meat, fish or poultry, satays have certain common denominators: all are immersed in a spicy, sweet-hot marinade, skewered, then grilled.

One caveat about leftover peanut sauce, which must be refrigerated: It will thicken rapidly when heated, so only warm the sauce to room temperature. You can thin it by adding a little broth. By the way, you don't *have* to fire up the grill to enjoy this zesty dish—the broiler will do just fine. Minted Carrot Toss, page 47, partners deliciously with this dish, and if you aren't fond of peanuts, try serving the satay with Gingered Mango Salsa, page 40. For a great sandwich, spread bread with peanut sauce, then top with leftover satay and thin slices of cucumber.

Serves 4 to 6

³/₄ cup beef or chicken broth

3 tablespoons rice wine vinegar

3 tablespoons soy sauce

3 tablespoons brown sugar

2 tablespoons minced fresh ginger

2 medium cloves garlic, minced

¹/₄–¹/₂ teaspoon crushed red pepper flakes

1¹/₂ pounds beef sirloin tip or boneless pork sirloin, cut into ¹/₄-inch-thick slices

1 cup unsalted dry-roasted peanuts

¹/₃ cup minced cilantro

Salt

In a large (about 13 by 9 inches), shallow glass or ceramic pan, combine broth, vinegar, soy sauce, sugar, ginger, garlic and pepper flakes. Add meat, turning to coat both sides. Cover tightly with plastic wrap; refrigerate at least 3 (preferably 8) hours. Once or twice during marinating time, spoon marinade over meat's surface. Or place meat and marinade in a large plastic bag, seal tightly and refrigerate, turning several times.

One hour before grilling the meat, remove it from refrigerator; if using bamboo skewers, soak them in water so they won't burn during cooking. Thread meat slices lengthwise onto metal or soaked bamboo skewers; cover and refrigerate until ready to cook. Pour marinade into a medium saucepan; bring to a boil. Cook at a full rolling boil for 3 minutes. Remove from heat; cool until lukewarm (turn mixture into a medium bowl for faster cooling).

Place peanuts, cilantro and cooled marinade mixture in a blender jar. Cover blender and process, beginning at low speed and gradually increasing to high, until smooth. Pour sauce into serving dish; salt to taste. Cover and let stand at room temperature until ready to serve.

Grill skewered meat over high heat for about 1½ minutes per side (or broil 3 inches from heat source for same amount of time). Serve skewers hot, accompanied with ginger-peanut sauce.

Using Fresh Ginger

The exotic flavor of fresh ginger is peppery, spicy and slightly sweet, entirely different from dried ground ginger. The gnarled and bumpy gingerroot is available in most supermarkets. Purchase roots that are firm, smooth-skinned, and smell fresh and spicy. Refrigerate, tightly wrapped, up to 3 weeks; use a sharp knife to peel away the thin brown skin just before using. If you can't find fresh ginger, substitute its seasoned form— pale pink slices of ginger, found in Asian markets and some supermarkets, or use candied ginger, rinsing off any sugar crystals. Either choice is superior to dried ground ginger.

Rip-Roaring Rib Eyes

A 1-inch-thick rib-eye steak (also called market steak) weighs about 12 ounces, which is fine for large appetites, but too much for smaller ones. For 6-ounce portions, simply cut the rib eyes crosswise in half. It's better to do that than use very thin-cut steaks that weigh less but won't be as juicy when cooked. Serve these spicy steaks with cooling Avocado Salsa to temper the heat.

*Makes 4 (12-ounce)
or 8 (6-ounce) servings*

3 medium cloves garlic, minced

1 teaspoon salt

1 tablespoon ground cumin

1 tablespoon good-quality chili powder

1/2 teaspoon cayenne pepper

1/2 teaspoon ground ginger

*4 (1-inch-thick) rib-eye steaks, trimmed of
 excess fat*

In a small bowl, combine garlic and salt. Use the back of a spoon to mash together until garlic is pulverized. Add cumin, chili powder, cayenne and ginger, mixing until well combined. Rub about 1/2 tablespoon spice mixture over both sides of each steak. Cover and refrigerate at least 2 hours.

These steaks can be cooked by a variety of methods. The following timing will produce medium-rare meat.

To panbroil: Heat a heavy, ungreased skillet over high heat until very hot. Add meat; cook on one side 4 minutes. Turn and cook other side 4 to 5 minutes.

To broil: Position rack 4 inches from broiling unit; preheat broiler. Cook meat 5 minutes on one side; turn and cook second side 4 to 5 minutes.

To grill: Soak 1 cup wood chips in water to cover at least 1 hour before beginning to cook; set and light the fire. When fire is ready, sprinkle the soaked wood chips over the heat source. Grill meat over a hot fire about 5 minutes on each side.

Avocado Salsa

2 tablespoons fresh lime juice

1 tablespoon olive oil

1 medium clove garlic, minced

1 small jalapeño pepper, seeded and minced, or 1 tablespoon minced canned jalapeño pepper

1/2 teaspoon good-quality chili powder

1/4 teaspoon salt

4 plum tomatoes (about 1/2 pound), seeded and diced

1/3 cup finely chopped jícama

1 scallion, green portion only, finely chopped

1–3 tablespoons minced fresh cilantro

2 medium-ripe but firm avocados, peeled, seeded and diced

In a medium bowl, whisk together lime juice, oil, garlic, jalapeño, chili powder and salt. Stir in tomatoes, jícama, scallion and cilantro. Add avocados, stirring only to incorporate so they don't get mushy. Cover tightly; refrigerate at least 2 hours. Makes about 2 cups.

Portly Flank Steak

As the name implies, this steak comes from the animal's lower hindquarters (the flank). It's lean and fibrous, and therefore benefits both from marinating overnight and brief cooking. The marinating medium here becomes the foundation for a seductive port-Gorgonzola sauce. I use tawny port in this recipe for its pale color and slightly nutty nuance. Know that if you use a vintage port or ruby port, both of which are deep purple-red in color, the sauce will take on a decidedly pink hue. Take care when cooking flank steak—it can turn from tender to leatherlike in less time than it takes to say, "I wish I hadn't overcooked it"! If you prefer your beef well done, choose another cut, like round steak; flank steak is best cooked medium rare.

Serves 4 to 6

1¹/₂ cups tawny port

¹/₂ cup tomato sauce

³/₄ cup finely chopped leeks, white
   portion only

3 medium cloves garlic, crushed

1 teaspoon coarsely ground black pepper

¹/₂ teaspoon ground allspice

¹/₂ teaspoon ground coriander

1 (1¹/₂-pound) flank steak, about
   ¹/₂ inch thick

1 cup beef broth

4 ounces Gorgonzola cheese, crumbled

Salt

In a large (about 13 by 9 inches), shallow glass or ceramic pan, stir together port, tomato sauce, leeks, garlic, pepper, allspice and coriander; set aside. Trim visible fat from flank steak. If necessary, pound meat so that it's approximately the same thickness (1/2 inch) all over. Use a sharp knife to score steak on each side in a diamond pattern, cutting about 1/8 inch deep. Dip meat in marinade to coat one side. Flip steak onto uncoated side in marinade. Cover tightly with plastic wrap; refrigerate 24 hours. Once or twice during marinating time, either turn steak over or spoon marinade over surface. *Or* place meat and marinade in a large plastic bag, seal tightly and refrigerate, turning several times.

At least 1 hour before grilling steak, soak 2 cups wood chips in water to cover; remove meat from refrigerator. When ready, light fire in outdoor grill according to manufacturer's directions. About 15 minutes before putting the meat on the grill, drain marinade into a medium saucepan. Bring to a boil; cook until the liquid is reduced by half, about 10 minutes. Add beef broth and bring back to a boil; reduce again by half. Put cheese in a blender jar; pour hot sauce over cheese. Cover blender and place your hand (protected by an oven mitt) over the cover. Beginning at low speed and gradually increasing to high, process until smooth. Return to saucepan; season to taste with salt. Cover and keep warm over low heat until meat is cooked.

Just before grilling, sprinkle soaked wood chips over heat source. Grill steak over high heat 3 to 5 minutes per side. Carve by cutting diagonally across the grain into thin slices. Serve immediately with port-Gorgonzola sauce.

Using Canned Broth in Recipes

Since there are two types of canned broth, it's important to know what kind you're using. *Condensed broth* requires the addition of water—using it undiluted usually produces a harsh, salty flavor. *Ready-to-serve broth* is recipe-ready. Fat-free broth is now available in most supermarkets. Or chill regular canned broth for several hours to congeal the fat, then lift it off before using the liquid.

Nutty Veal Niçoise

This dish is easy, impressive and fast —cooking time is only about 10 minutes. Veal scallops are small, oval, boneless slices, usually from the leg. My butcher cuts them so they're about 1/8 inch thick and weigh 3 ounces each. Put larger scallops between two pieces of plastic wrap or waxed paper and pound gently with the flat side of a mallet, or flatten with a rolling pin to a thickness of 1/8 to 1/4 inch—be careful not to tear the flesh. If fresh tomatoes aren't ripe and flavorful, it's far better to use one (14 1/2-ounce) can of ready-cut tomatoes.

Serves 6

12 veal scallops
Salt and freshly ground black pepper
6 tablespoons olive oil or half oil, half
    unsalted butter
2 medium cloves garlic, minced
Finely grated zest from 1 medium lemon
3 medium tomatoes, seeded and finely
    chopped (about 1 1/2 cups)
2 tablespoons lemon juice
1/3 cup Niçoise olives, pitted and coarsely
    chopped
1/4 cup finely chopped scallions, green
    portion only
1/2 cup finely chopped fresh basil leaves or
    2 1/2 tablespoons dried basil, crumbled
1/2 cup finely chopped, well-toasted
    walnuts

Salt and pepper veal to taste. In a large skillet, heat 3 tablespoons oil over medium-high heat. Sauté veal 2 to 3 minutes per side, depending on the thickness. Transfer scallops to a warm platter; cover and keep warm while cooking sauce.

To same skillet, add remaining 3 tablespoons oil, garlic and lemon zest. Cook over medium-high heat, stirring often, for 1 minute. Stir in tomatoes, lemon juice and olives; cook 3 minutes. Add scallions; cook 1 minute. Remove from heat; stir in basil. Salt and pepper to taste. Spoon over veal scallops; sprinkle with walnuts.

Memorable Meatballs

If there's such a thing as multipurpose meatballs, here they are. They're tender and moist and slightly spicy—great alone, in a sandwich or combined with marinara sauce for pasta. Leftovers make excellent hash. Tiny 1-inch versions are terrific served with cocktails. Make a double batch and freeze one for a future meal in minutes. Cheddar, Monterey Jack or any other firm cheese can be substituted for the provolone.

Serves 6 to 8

1 (8-ounce) can tomato sauce
1/2 cup fresh bread crumbs
1/2 cup finely chopped green bell pepper
1 cup grated provolone cheese (4 ounces)
1 medium clove garlic, minced
3/4 teaspoon salt
1/4 teaspoon ground nutmeg
1/4–1/2 teaspoon cayenne pepper
1 pound lean ground beef
1 pound lean ground pork

In a large bowl, combine tomato sauce, bread crumbs, bell pepper, provolone, garlic, salt, nutmeg and cayenne; mix well. Add beef and pork; knead together until thoroughly combined. Shape into 38 (1½-inch) meatballs. Cover and refrigerate until ready to cook.

In a large skillet over medium-high heat, cook meatballs until well browned on all sides, about 10 minutes. Serve hot.

Tips on Ground Meat

■ Because fat provides moistness and therefore tenderness, leaner ground meat produces dryer burgers, meat loaves and meatballs. Ground meat, in order of leanest to fattest, generally ranges as follows: ground sirloin contains between 12 and 15 percent fat; ground round, between 20 and 23 percent; ground chuck, from 23 to 30 percent; and regular ground beef usually contains about 30 percent. Keep in mind that the fat content as well as the name of a particular grind of meat may vary from market to market, so check the label. It should tell you the percentage of fat or, conversely, that of lean.

■ There will be more shrinkage in meat with a higher fat content than in lean meat.

■ Coarsely ground meat produces a moister, more tender end product than finely ground meat.

■ If you're using lean meat because you want to avoid animal fat, you can replenish some of the moisture by mixing in 1 to 2 tablespoons vegetable oil per pound of ground meat. Or add 2 to 3 tablespoons of meat or vegetable broth, tomato juice, wine, beer or other liquid to each pound of meat.

Meatball Tips

■ For information on buying ground meat and combining ingredients, see Meat Loaf Tips, page 101.

■ To form 1½-inch meatballs quickly and evenly, shape mixture into a log 1½ inches in diameter, then cut into 1½-inch lengths and roll each piece into a ball.

■ A small ice cream scoop or a ⅛- to ¼-cup measure is good for shaping uniform meatballs.

■ Dampen your hands with cold water before forming meatballs to keep the meat from sticking to your fingers.

■ Use a gentle touch when shaping meatballs or the mixture may fall apart. On the other hand, an overhandled mixture can become too compacted, resulting in an overly dense meatball.

■ Put a ½-inch chunk of cheese in the center of each meatball, closing the meat around it. By the time the meatballs are cooked, the cheese will have melted and ooze out as you bite into them.

Meatball Muffuletta

A specialty of New Orleans, the classic muffuletta (pronounced moof-fuh-LEHT-tuh, and also spelled muffaletta), is a hero-style sandwich of ham, Genoa salami, provolone and a piquant Creole-Italian creation called olive salad, which aficionados say *makes* a muffuletta. Though the meatball variation was my idea, for the olive salad recipe I turned to my good friend and favorite New Orleansian, Dick Brennan, Jr., managing partner of the famed Commander's Palace restaurant. I like to make these sandwiches with hot meatballs, but they're still enticing made ahead of time and served cold or at room temperature.

Serves 6 to 8

Dickie Brennan's Olive Salad, page 38
Memorable Meatballs, page 35
2 round Italian or French loaves, 8 inches
    in diameter and 2 inches high, or 6 to
    8 oblong Italian or French rolls, cut in
    half lengthwise
3/4 pound sliced provolone cheese

A day (or at least several hours) before you plan to make meatball muffulettas, prepare the olive salad and refrigerate. If making salad only a few hours in advance, let it stand at room temperature.

Prepare meatballs (they may be made in advance and served cold or at room temperature or reheated). While meatballs are cooking (if you're making them just before serving), brush cut sides of bread with some of the dressing from the olive salad. Divide provolone slices evenly between bottom halves of bread. Drain meatballs on paper towels; place hot meatballs atop cheese. Spoon olive salad evenly over meatballs, using about 1⅓ cups each for the large loaves, ⅓ cup each for the rolls. Position top halves of bread on top of meatballs and cheese, pressing down slightly before cutting large loaves into quarters, and rolls into halves.

America is a confirmed sandwich nation.

—James Beard

Dickie Brennan's Olive Salad

This recipe looks long, but it's definitely worth the effort. If you *must* take a shortcut, substitute 2½ cups *giardiniera* (mixed pickled vegetables, found in Italian markets and supermarkets) for the celery, carrots, cauliflower, onions and bell peppers. Peperoncini (also called Tuscan peppers) are slightly sweet chiles that can range from medium to medium-hot. They are found in jars in the condiment or ethnic-food section of most supermarkets.

Make the olive salad a day in advance so the flavors have time to marry and mingle. Leftover olive salad can be tightly sealed and refrigerated for up to 2 weeks. Use it finely chopped to top bruschetta, mix into mashed potatoes, toss with salad greens, blend with cream cheese for a spread . . . well, you get the idea.

Makes about 5 cups

¾ cup olive oil

2 teaspoons white wine vinegar

⅓ cup finely chopped parsley

6 medium cloves garlic, minced

1 teaspoon freshly ground black pepper

1½ tablespoons minced fresh oregano or
   2 teaspoons dried leaf oregano,
   crumbled

2 tablespoons drained, finely chopped,
   seeded and stemmed peperoncini

1 tablespoon capers

½ cup halved, pitted Spanish olives

½ cup halved, pitted Greek (calamata)
   olives

½ cup thinly sliced celery

½ cup thinly sliced carrots

½ cup finely chopped pickled cauliflower

½ cup marinated cocktail onions,
   drained

½ cup diced red bell pepper

Salt (optional)

In a large ceramic or glass bowl, combine olive oil, vinegar, parsley, garlic, pepper, oregano, peperoncini and capers; whisk until well combined. Add all remaining ingredients except salt; toss to thoroughly coat vegetables with dressing.

Taste; if not piquant enough, add 1 to 2 tablespoons olive brine. Cover tightly and refrigerate overnight. Adjust seasoning with salt, if necessary. Serve at room temperature.

Getting a Handle on Herbs—Fresh Versus Dry

There's no doubt about it—fresh herbs have flavor and freshness their dried counterparts simply can't match. There are times, however, when fresh herbs are simply not available. When that happens, the substitution ratio is 1 (of dried herbs) to 3 (of fresh herbs). Otherwise, if a recipe calls for 3 teaspoons (1 tablespoon) fresh herbs, substitute 1 teaspoon dried herbs. Conversely, if a recipe calls for 1 teaspoon dried herbs, the fresh herb equivalent is 3 teaspoons.

Gingered Mango Pork Loin

I love this Gingered Mango Salsa so much that I usually double the recipe. You can use it in myriad ways: in pork or chicken sandwiches; tossed with chunks of cold leftover meat as a salad; stirred into a salad dressing; and as a last-minute mix-in for stir-fries. Paper-thin slices of pale pink seasoned ginger can be found in Asian markets as well as in the ethnic-food section of some supermarkets. If you can't find it, substitute 2 tablespoons minced fresh ginger. If fresh mangoes are out of season, look for frozen mango. Some markets also carry mango slices in jars.

Serves 8 to 10

Gingered Mango Salsa

1 medium mango, peeled, seeded and diced (about 1 heaping cup)
1 large ripe tomato, seeded and diced (about 1 heaping cup)
1 jalapeño pepper, seeded and minced
2 tablespoons seasoned sliced ginger, drained and finely chopped
2 tablespoons finely chopped fresh mint
1 tablespoon fresh lime juice
Salt

Pork

1 tablespoon olive oil
1 large clove garlic, minced
1 teaspoon good-quality chili powder
1/2 teaspoon ground cinnamon
1/2 teaspoon salt
1 boneless pork loin (4 to 4 1/2 pounds), trimmed of excess fat

Gingered Mango Salsa

In a medium bowl, combine mango, tomato, jalapeño, ginger, mint and lime juice. Cover and refrigerate at least 1 hour for flavors to blend. Taste before serving and salt if necessary. Let stand at room temperature for 30 minutes before serving. Refrigerate leftover salsa. Makes about 2 cups.

Pork

Position oven rack in the middle of the oven. Preheat oven to 350°F. In a small bowl, combine oil, garlic, chili powder, cinnamon and salt, stirring to form a paste. Rub into surface of pork loin. Place meat in a shallow roasting pan. Roast, uncovered, for about 1½ hours, or until pork reaches an internal temperature of 155°F on a meat thermometer. Lightly brush meat's surface with olive oil twice (at half-hour intervals) during roasting time.

Remove roast from oven and let stand 15 minutes before carving. Serve with Gingered Mango Salsa.

Working with Chiles

The seeds and membranes of a chile pepper can contain up to 80 percent of the potent compound (capsaicin) that gives a chile its fiery nature. It's the capsaicin that can also cause severe skin and eye irritation on contact. That's why it's important that you handle chiles with care (try not to touch the seeds and membranes), and wash your hands thoroughly with hot water and soap after you're through working with them. For fail-safe, pain-free chile handling, wear rubber kitchen gloves or the thin plastic disposable gloves available in drugstores and hardware stores.

Plum Crazy Pork Chops

This sweet-and-snappy plum sauce complements pork perfectly, but is equally delicious with duck. It's the creation of my dear friend and consummate cook Glenn Miwa, owner-chef of the wonderful Comforts restaurant in San Anselmo, California. The addition of allspice is my contrivance—food writers can never leave recipes alone (not even their own).

Serves 6

1 (12-ounce) jar plum preserves, preferably damson (about 1½ cups)

1 (12-ounce) bottle hearty beer or ale (1½ cups)

⅓ cup Worcestershire sauce

¼ cup cider vinegar

3 medium cloves garlic, minced

2 teaspoons Dijon mustard

½–1 teaspoon hot pepper sauce

½ teaspoon ground allspice

Salt and freshly ground black pepper

2 tablespoons olive oil

6 center-cut loin pork chops, about 1½ inches thick

Finely chop any large pieces of fruit in the preserves. Combine all ingredients except salt and pepper, olive oil and chops in a medium saucepan. Bring to a full rolling boil over high heat. Reduce heat to medium low; cook, uncovered, until sauce thickly coats a metal spoon and has reduced to about 1½ cups, about 40 minutes. Salt and pepper to taste. If possible, refrigerate sauce overnight for flavors to mellow.

Trim any excess fat from pork chops; season meat on both sides with salt and pepper. Heat 1 tablespoon oil in each of two large skillets over medium-high heat. Brown chops (3 in each skillet) on each side, about 4 minutes per side. Reduce heat to medium low; pour hot sauce over chops, evenly dividing it between the two skillets; if sauce has been refrigerated, warm it in the microwave oven for 1 minute on HIGH (100 percent power). Cover and cook about 6 minutes. Flip chops and continue cooking about 6 minutes, or until done to your preference (160°F on a meat thermometer delivers tender, juicy meat). Serve hot, topped with sauce.

Don't Think It Won't Make a Difference

Wine, beer and liquor can add incomparable intrigue to many dishes. That is, of course, if you use a *quality* potable. When cooking with such liquids, *never* use anything you wouldn't happily drink. But that caveat goes even further. Even though you might drink so-called light beer for its low-calorie allure, forget about using it in a recipe that calls for a bold-flavored dark beer—any flavor it delivers will be lackluster at best. It's preferable to buy a single bottle of a good, full-flavored beer than to use something that won't contribute flavor. And, I implore you, never (but never!) use the "cooking wine" commonly found in supermarkets—the deplorable flavor can ruin a dish. Cooking a sauce reduces it (because some of the moisture evaporates), which intensifies the flavor. When that happens with an inferior potable, the flavor just gets worse.

Rumrunners' Ribs

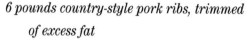

My friend Lee Janvrin said I ought to call these ribs "damn good ribs." This recipe departs from the norm in that the ribs are first boiled to render much of their fat, then immersed overnight in a sauce redolent of rum, molasses, ginger and orange zest. It's equally good made with bourbon. Save the rich liquid after the ribs are boiled—cool it to room temperature, refrigerate until the fat congeals, then lift off and discard the solidified fat. The resulting stock can be frozen and used later as a base for soups or sauces.

Serves 6 to 8

6 pounds country-style pork ribs, trimmed of excess fat

2 tablespoons olive oil

1 large onion, finely chopped

4 medium cloves garlic, minced

2/3 cup red wine vinegar

2/3 cup unsulfured molasses

2 (8-ounce) cans tomato sauce

2 cups rum, preferably dark

Finely grated zest of 2 large oranges

3 tablespoons minced ginger

2 teaspoons freshly ground black pepper

1 teaspoon ground allspice

Salt

Place ribs in a large Dutch oven or other heavy pot; cover with water. Bring to a boil. Cover and cook at a slow boil for about 45 minutes, or until pork is fork-tender.

While ribs are cooking, prepare sauce. Heat oil in a large skillet over medium-high heat; sauté onion until well browned, about 10 minutes. Add garlic; sauté 2 minutes. Stir in all remaining ingredients except salt; bring to a boil. Reduce heat to medium low; cook, uncovered, for 15 minutes. Salt to taste. Pour sauce into a large, shallow glass or ceramic dish. Use a slotted spoon to transfer ribs from their cooking liquid to sauce.

Spoon some of the sauce over the ribs. Cover tightly; refrigerate overnight.

At least 1 hour before grilling ribs, soak 2 cups wood chips in water to cover; remove meat from refrigerator. When ready, light fire in outdoor grill according to manufacturer's directions. Wait until fire is relatively low (see pages 19–20) before beginning to cook ribs. Just before beginning to grill, sprinkle drained wood chips over heat source.

Shake sauce off ribs. Put ribs on grill; cover and cook for 30 minutes, turning halfway through. Just before ribs are done, heat sauce until hot. Serve sauce with ribs.

If you want a subject, look to pork!
—Charles Dickens, *Great Expectations*

Tomato Sauce Substitute

I always keep tomato paste in a tube on hand—it's small, easy to store and lasts a long time. It can also be substituted for tomato sauce in a pinch. Simply combine $^3/_8$ cup tomato paste with $^1/_2$ cup water, and you have the equivalent of 1 cup tomato sauce.

Moroccan Lamb Skewers

This recipe is my version of *kefta,* a spiced, finely ground meat mixture that in Morocco is generally skewered and grilled. The meat should be finely ground in order to hold together on the skewers. You'll need four 12-inch skewers, either metal or wood; both can be found in cookware shops, hardware stores and some supermarkets. Metal skewers are easier to work with and are reusable, but if you prefer bamboo skewers, soak them in water *at least* 1 hour before using so they won't burn up on the grill. The meat can also be broiled or sautéed off the skewers, as well as shaped into a smaller size for appetizers. Serve it with warm pita bread and Minted Carrot Toss (recipe follows). A rice pilaf is an ideal accompaniment.

Serves 4

¹⁄₂ cup fresh bread crumbs

¹⁄₄ cup milk

1 egg, lightly beaten

1 pound finely ground lamb

2 tablespoons minced fresh mint

1 tablespoon minced fresh ginger

1 medium clove garlic, minced

¹⁄₂ teaspoon ground cumin

¹⁄₂ teaspoon freshly ground black pepper

¹⁄₂ teaspoon salt

¹⁄₄ teaspoon cayenne pepper

¹⁄₈ teaspoon each ground allspice, cardamom, cinnamon, cloves and nutmeg

In a large bowl, combine bread crumbs and milk; let stand 5 minutes. Add egg, stir well to combine. Add remaining ingredients; knead mixture until thoroughly combined. *Or* place soaked crumbs and remaining ingredients in a food processor fitted with the metal blade. Process until the mixture is well blended and smooth. Cover and refrigerate for at least 1 hour before cooking.

One hour before grilling the meat, soak 2 cups wood chips in water to cover. When ready, light fire in outdoor grill according to manufacturer's directions. Just before beginning to grill, sprinkle drained wood chips over heat source.

While fire is heating, form meat mixture into 12 (3-inch-long) *firmly* compacted sausage shapes. Spear three "sausages," end to end, on each of 4 metal skewers, allowing about 1/2 inch between them. Grill 6 to 8 minutes (for medium to well done), turning every 2 minutes or so to brown meat on all sides. Serve hot with warm pita bread and Minted Carrot Toss.

Minted Carrot Toss
Makes about 2 1/2 cups

2 tablespoons fresh lemon juice

2 tablespoons sugar

1/2 teaspoon ground cinnamon

Finely grated zest of 1 medium lemon

2 1/2 cups finely grated carrots
   (about 2 medium)

1/4 packed cup finely chopped fresh mint

Salt and freshly ground black pepper

In a medium bowl, combine lemon juice, sugar, cinnamon and lemon zest; stir well, mashing lemon zest against side of bowl to release citrus oils. Add carrots and mint, tossing to thoroughly coat with lemon mixture. Salt and pepper to taste. Cover and refrigerate for at least 2 hours before serving. Best if allowed to stand at room temperature for 30 minutes before serving.

Fresh Bread Crumbs

Besides having a better flavor, fresh bread crumbs don't absorb as much liquid as their dried counterparts. To make your own fresh bread crumbs, lightly toast slices of bread, then tear them into pieces and put in a food processor fitted with the metal blade. Process with quick ON/OFF pulses until the crumbs reach the desired texture. A blender can handle only 2 slices at a time, but also produces good results. One regular untrimmed slice of bread yields about 1/2 cup crumbs.

French Lamb Chops with Minted Onion Marmalade

The small French chops come from the rib section also known as the "rack of lamb," and have had the fatty meat trimmed away from the end of the bone. The double French chops (2 ribs per chop) make an elegant presentation and provide just enough meat for an average appetite. The lamb can be prepared in almost any manner, but I think the slightly smoky flavor of grilled chops is particularly nice with the marmalade.

Although I created the Minted Onion Marmalade to go with lamb chops, it has myriad uses. One favorite is spreading a thick layer on good French bread and topping it with slices of vine-ripened tomatoes, sprinkled with salt and pepper. I've even combined it with olive oil and vinegar and whirled it in a blender to make a delicious salad dressing. Prepare the marmalade a day before you plan to serve it to let the flavors blend and deepen.

Serves 6

Minted Onion Marmalade

2 tablespoons olive oil

1 1/2 pounds white onions, thinly sliced (1/8 inch thick), then randomly cut in quarters

1 tablespoon sugar

2 medium cloves garlic, minced

1/2 cup dry sherry

1/4 teaspoon salt

1 teaspoon balsamic vinegar

Finely grated zest of 1 large lemon

1 cup packed fresh mint leaves, finely chopped

Lamb Chops

6 double-cut French lamb chops

Salt and freshly ground black pepper to taste

5 mint sprigs (optional)

Minted Onion Marmalade

Heat oil in a large skillet over medium-high heat. Sauté onions, stirring occasionally, for 10 minutes. Sprinkle sugar over onions. Reduce heat to medium; sauté for 10 more minutes. Stir in garlic, sherry, salt, vinegar and all but 1 teaspoon of the lemon zest. Cover and cook, stirring 2 to 3 times, for 10 minutes, or until liquid is absorbed. Remove from heat; cool to room temperature. Stir in mint and remaining teaspoon of lemon zest. Cover and refrigerate overnight. Serve at room temperature. Makes about 1¼ cups.

Lamb Chops

Salt and pepper both sides of meat to taste. Cook lamb by any of the following methods; all will produce medium-rare meat (for medium, add 1 minute cooking time to each side).

To grill: Soak 1 cup wood chips in water to cover at least 1 hour before beginning to cook; set and light the fire. When fire is ready, sprinkle the soaked wood chips over the heat source. Grill meat about 5 minutes on each side.

To panbroil: Heat a heavy, ungreased skillet over high heat until very hot. Add meat; cook on one side 4 minutes. Turn and cook other side 4 to 5 minutes.

To broil: Position rack 4 inches from broiling unit; preheat broiler. Cook meat 5 minutes on one side; turn and cook second side 4 to 5 minutes.

Serve lamb accompanied by Minted Onion Marmalade, garnished with mint sprigs, if desired.

Potatoes

One Potato, Two Potato ... the Six Basic Types

Although there are hundreds of potato varieties, the great majority of those grown in the United States come from just six basic types—four regular (or common) and two sweet. In the regular potato category are russets, long whites, round whites and round reds; sweet potatoes include pale- and dark-fleshed varieties. To add to the confusion, potatoes are often marketed under the name of the geographic location where they were grown —such as California, Idaho, Long Island or Maine. Following are descriptions of the six basic potato types.

Russet potatoes (also called *old potatoes, baking potatoes* or sometimes simply *Idaho potatoes* (after the state leading in production). They have an elliptical shape and numerous eyes. Their skin is rough and brown, their flesh white with a cooked texture that's somewhat dry and mealy. Russets have a low-moisture and high-starch content, making them excellent for baking, mashing and frying. Varieties include *Russet Burbank, Russet Arcadia* and *Butte*.

Long white potatoes (often marketed as *all-purpose potatoes*) are also elongated in shape, though typically somewhat flatter than russets. They have an extremely thin, pale tan-colored skin and a white flesh that's firm and *slightly* waxy. Depending on the variety, the eyes can range from fairly deep-set to almost imperceptible. Long whites have a medium starch content that makes them good for boiling, frying, roasting or steaming. Varieties include *Kennebec, Sebago* and *White Rose.*

Round red potatoes (sometimes labeled *boiling potatoes*) range in shape from round to slightly oblong and in size from small to medium. Depending on the variety, their thin skin may vary in color from medium to dark red, their eyes from deep to shallow. Round red potatoes have a waxy, high-moisture white flesh. Their starch content ranges from medium to medium low, making them best for boiling, gratins, roasting and steaming. Varieties include *LaRouge, Red LaSoda* and *Red Pontiac.*

Round white potatoes (also marketed as *boiling potatoes*) are round and have a thin, pale tan-colored skin with shallow to medium eyes. They range in size from small to medium, and have a medium-starch, high-moisture, waxy white flesh. Round whites are good for boiling, gratins, roasting and steaming. Varieties include *Katahdin* and *Superior.*

New potatoes are *not* a specific variety but, rather, the youngsters of any member of the regular potato clan, primarily those harvested from green vines in the spring and throughout the summer. Because they're freshly dug and immature, new potatoes are small in size and have thin, undeveloped wispy skins. Their relatively low-starch flesh is waxy, their flavor sweet, making them excellent for boiling or roasting. Since they retain their shape after being cooked and cut or sliced, new potatoes are a good choice for potato salads.

Sweet potatoes are rather large, irregularly shaped, generally oblong tubers that are actually members of the morning glory family. Though there are hundreds of sweet potato varieties, they fall into two broad categories: pale- and dark-fleshed, the latter often erroneously labeled "yams" in American markets, although true yams typically need a tropical climate in which to grow. **Pale-fleshed sweet potatoes** have a thin, tan to light brown skin, and a flesh that ranges in color from light to medium yellow. Their cooked texture is dry and crumbly, much like that of a regular baking potato, and their flavor is faintly sweet. **Dark-fleshed sweet potatoes** have a thicker, tougher skin that can range in color from red-orange to copper to a dark reddish brown. Their flesh, usually a vivid bright to deep orange hue, is sweet, moist and typically finely grained.

Others in the Field—Specialty Potatoes

Specialty produce markets, farmer's markets and even some supermarkets carry a range of interesting, appealing specialty potatoes that are far from traditional. Excellent flavors and textures can be found in tubers that range in color from bright red to blue to almost black.

Blue and purple potatoes are typically small and vary in shape from oval to round. Their thin skins can range from indigo blue to purple-black, and their flesh from dark blue to purple (some with white streaks). These potatoes are high in moisture, making them good for boiling and roasting. Varieties include *All Blue* and *Purple Peruvian.* You can also find potatoes with deep purple skins and white flesh, such as the *Caribe* and *Purple Chief,* both of which make fluffy, moist mashed potatoes.

Fingerling potatoes are small and stubby, and their skins range in color from buff to pinkish bronze. Fingerlings have a subtly sweet, pale yellow flesh that's firm and waxy, making them good candidates for boiling and roasting. Some of the more readily available varieties are *German Yellow, Rose Finn, Ruby Crescent* and *Russian Banana.*

Red- and pink-fleshed potatoes are typically medium-size, round to oblong specimens with a range in skin color from red to maroon and a flesh that varies from pink to red. Some, like the *Huckleberry,* have a red flesh marbled with white. Like blue potatoes, red-fleshed varieties are good for boiling and roasting.

Yellow-fleshed potatoes (the most popular of which are *Bintje, Butterball, Yellow Finn* and *Yukon Gold*) are generally round and vary in size from small to medium. Their skins range in color from light tan to light brown, and their waxy flesh from pale to deep yellow. Most of these potatoes are known for their rich, sweet flavor; the Yellow Finn is particularly noted for its sweetness, the Butterball for its buttery texture. Yellow-fleshed potatoes are multi-purpose, and are especially good for boiling, frying, gratins, mashing and roasting.

Excellent potatoes, smoking hot, and accompanied by melted butter of the first quality, would alone stamp merit on any dinner....

—Thomas Walker, *The Original,* 1835

Food for Thought

It's been said before and certainly bears repeating: It's not the potato that's fattening, it's what you put on it (like butter, sour cream and bacon). Not only is the humble potato fat- and cholesterol-free and highly digestible, but it packs a powerhouse punch of nutrition. Of course, as with most food, some preparation methods deliver more of nature's dividend than others. For example, a potato's skin (and the flesh just beneath it) is particularly nutrient-rich, so cooking potatoes unpeeled is simply being nutrition-smart. (You can always peel them after cooking.) Likewise, potatoes cooked in water will give up much of their nutritional goodness to the liquid (one reason to save and use the cooking water). And consider this: The calorie count of a potato can triple when you fry it.

The nutritional stats: A medium (5.5-ounce) russet potato contains a modest 120 calories, 27 grams of carbohydrates (mostly complex), 3 grams of protein and only a trace of sodium. It embodies a prodigious amount of vitamin C (40 percent of the daily requirement) plus vitamin B_6, niacin (B_3), pantothenic acid, riboflavin (B_2), thiamin (B_1), and the minerals copper, iron, magnesium, potassium, phosphorus and zinc.

A small (5-ounce) sweet potato, which weighs in at around 160 calories, doesn't have as much protein, phosphorus, potassium or niacin as its nonsweet counterpart, but is a good source of vitamin E and packs a nutritional wallop: Its vitamin A content provides almost 70 percent of the recommended daily allowance. One cup of cooked sweet potato contains more vitamin A than 23 cups of broccoli.

Buying and Storing Potatoes

Buying Potatoes

Choose varieties that are firm, well-shaped for their type and blemish-free. Avoid specimens that are wrinkled, sprouted, cracked or that have soft spots. A slight green tinge on regular potatoes is indicative of prolonged light exposure, which produces solanine, an alkaloid that can be toxic if eaten in quantity. The potato can be used if this bitter green portion is cut away or scraped off. Select potatoes that are relatively the same size so they'll cook evenly and get done at the same time.

Storing Potatoes (regular and sweet)

Warm temperatures encourage sprouting and shriveling, so choose a cool, dark, well-ventilated place in which to store potatoes—up to 2 weeks for regular potatoes, about 1 week for sweet potatoes. If the temperature of the storage area is around 50°F, regular potatoes will keep up to 3 months, sweets up to 1 month. Refrigeration causes potatoes to become overly sweet and/or turn dark when cooked. *New potatoes* are highly perishable and should be used within a week of purchase (unless stored under ideal conditions at 50°F, in which case they can last up to a month). Potatoes need good air circulation and are best stored in a paper or net bag or in a basket. Storing them in a plastic bag will hasten spoilage. Don't store potatoes near onions or apples, both of which contain ethylene gas, which speeds sprouting and spoilage.

Freezing Potatoes

Potatoes can be frozen with varying degrees of success. Leftover mashed potatoes can be frozen up to 1 month. Other potatoes intended for freezing should be partially cooked first by blanching—1 minute for shredded potatoes, 2 to 3 minutes (depending on thickness) for potato slices or sticks to be French-fried or oven-roasted. Plunge blanched potatoes into ice water to stop the cooking immediately. Blot dry and freeze in vaporproof wrapping up to 2 months. Frozen potatoes can be cooked from their frozen state, or defrosted then cooked. The most unsuccessfully frozen potatoes are those in liquids (like soups), which have a tendency to fall apart when reheated.

Choose Potatoes by How They'll Be Used

- *For baking:* russets and Yukon golds

- *For boiling (as for salads):* long whites, round reds and whites, Yukon golds

- *For frying:* russets, long whites and Yukon golds

- *For gratins and scalloped dishes:* long whites, round reds and whites, Yukon golds

- *For mashing:* russets and Yukon golds

- *For roasting:* long whites, round reds and whites, small Yukon golds

- *For soups and stews:* russets, Yukon golds

- *For steaming:* long whites, round reds and whites

What I say is that, if a fellow really likes potatoes,
he must be a pretty decent sort of fellow.

—A. A. Milne

General Tips on Potatoes and Sweet Potatoes

Regular Potatoes

• Before peeling a potato, remember, the skin is rich both in flavor and nutrients.

• If you do peel potatoes, remove as thin a layer as possible—much of the flavor is found just below the skin.

• Use a vegetable brush to thoroughly scrub potatoes that will be cooked with the skin on.

• Even if you don't want to cook potatoes with their peels on, you can have the best of both worlds by scrubbing the potato, peeling it, then saving the peel (freeze, if necessary) for future use. Potato peels can be fried (or oven-crisped) and eaten plain as a snack, or used to scoop up dips, or crumbled over salads or mashed potatoes. Cut them into small pieces or puree them to use for flavoring soups, stews, sauces and so on.

• The flesh of potatoes darkens when exposed to air, so if you must cut them ahead of time, dip them in a mixture of 1 quart cool water and 3 tablespoons lemon juice. Drain well, then cover and refrigerate until ready to use.

• If the soaked potatoes are to be fried, thoroughly blot them dry with paper towels before adding them to the fat.

- If potato flesh has darkened, cooking them in milk rewhitens them (but don't let the milk boil). After cooling, the flavored milk can be refrigerated up to 3 days to use in sauces, soups, etc.

- A teaspoon or two of lemon juice in the cooking water keeps potatoes white after they're cooked.

- Potato skins are easier to remove while the potatoes are still hot.

- When cooking potatoes that are to be mashed, leave the skins on. Peel the cooked potatoes, returning the skins to the water. Cool, purée and freeze this flavorful liquid for future use.

- After boiling potatoes, use the nutritious, flavorful water for soups, sauces or as the liquid in breads.

- Get a jump on the next night's meal by cooking twice as many potatoes as you need for one meal. Use leftovers in salad, hash or soup, toss with other vegetables, or mash them.

Sweet Potatoes

- Pale-fleshed sweet potatoes can be substituted for regular potatoes in most recipes.

- When cutting a sweet potato, always use a stainless steel knife—carbon blades cause the flesh to darken.

- Sweet potatoes are more nutritious if cooked in their skins.

- Before baking or microwaving a sweet potato, pierce the skin with the tines of a fork.

- After peeling raw sweet potatoes, keep them from turning dark by soaking in cold acidulated water (1 quart of water mixed with 3 tablespoons lemon juice) for a few minutes. Drain well before using.

- Peeling boiled sweet potatoes is easy— just drain off the hot water, then immediately plunge the potatoes into cold water. The skins will pull right off.

- Another easy way to peel sweet potatoes is to cook, cool, then halve and scoop out the pulp with a spoon.

Potatoes are to food what sensible shoes are to fashion.

—Linda Wells, food writer

Potatoes

Skordalia

Pronounced *skor-dahl-YAH,* this garlicky Greek preparation is used as both a sauce for fish, poultry or vegetables, and a dip for crudités, bread and so forth. The everyday version is based on bread, but I prefer this potato rendition. The mint is nontraditional, but adds visual and flavor excitement, and the nuts contribute a wonderfully earthy nuance. Walnuts or pistachios can be substituted for the almonds, if you prefer. Remember, all nuts taste better toasted, a process that accentuates their flavor. If you don't have a food processor, finely chop the garlic and almonds, then use an electric mixer to blend the ingredients.

Makes about 4 cups

4 medium cloves garlic, peeled

1 cup well-toasted slivered almonds

1 pound russet potatoes, cooked, cooled, peeled and cut into eighths

1/8–1/4 teaspoon cayenne pepper

1/2 cup olive oil

1/4 cup fresh lemon juice

2 tablespoons red wine vinegar

1/2–1 1/2 cups vegetable or chicken broth

1/4 cup packed fresh mint leaves, finely chopped

Salt and freshly ground black pepper

1 tablespoon finely chopped fresh mint for garnish (optional)

With the machine running, drop the garlic cloves one by one into a food processor fitted with the metal blade. Process until garlic is chopped and clinging to sides of bowl. Scrape down sides of food processor bowl. Add almonds; process until very finely ground. Scrape down sides of bowl if necessary. Add potatoes, cayenne, olive oil, lemon juice and vinegar; process just until smooth, scraping down sides of bowl as necessary. Stir in enough broth to make the mixture medium thick; the amount of broth depends on the type of potatoes used. Stir in mint, and salt and pepper to taste. Serve at room temperature. If desired, sprinkle with 1 tablespoon chopped mint just before serving. May be covered and refrigerated up to 1 week.

Toasting Nuts

The flavor of any type of nut is intensified by toasting. The quickest way to toast nuts is to cook them in an ungreased skillet over medium-high heat and stir or toss them often until golden brown. Or toast nuts in a 350°F oven, stirring occasionally, for 10 to 15 minutes. Or place 1 cup of nuts on a paper plate and microwave at HIGH (100 percent power), for 3 to 4 minutes. Microwave-toasted nuts won't brown, but they'll smell and taste toasted. Cool toasted nuts before adding to recipes.

… a diet which consists predominantly of potatoes leads to the use of liquor.

—Friedrich Nietzsche

Pita Crisps

These chips are perfect dippers for Skordalia (page 60), and make deliciously crispy partners for soups or salads.

Makes about 6 dozen chips

3 pita breads, about 7 inches in diameter
2–3 tablespoons olive oil
Salt and freshly ground black pepper

Preheat oven to 350°F. Using a pointed knife, carefully separate pitas in half horizontally so you have 2 rounds from each pita. Lightly brush the inside of each round with oil; salt and pepper to taste. Stack pita rounds on top of each other. Use a sharp knife to cut pita stack into 12 pie-shaped wedges. Arrange wedges in a single layer, evenly spaced on 2 large, ungreased baking sheets. Bake 8 to 10 to 15 minutes, or until golden brown. Halfway through baking time, switch baking sheets from top to bottom, and turn from front to back to allow for oven hot spots. Remove from oven; cool on paper towels. Store chips in tightly sealed plastic bags up to 5 days. If necessary, recrisp chips in 350°F oven for 5 minutes.

A Word About Leeks

Buy leeks that are crisp and firm with no sign of withering or spotting on the leaves. Refrigerate them in a plastic bag up to 5 days. Because dirt can become trapped between the multiple layers of a leek, it's important to clean them thoroughly. To do so, slit the leek in half lengthwise and hold each half under cold, running water to flush out any soil.

Creamy Blue-Potato Bisque

No, the potatoes aren't blue (although there *are* blue potatoes). The "blue" in the title refers to the cheese with which this bisque is so subtly flavored. I use Cambozola, but any creamy blue cheese may be substituted. This soup is equally delicious hot or cold.

Serves 6 to 8

1 medium leek (white portion only),
　　finely chopped
1 tablespoon olive oil
1 medium clove garlic, minced
5 cups vegetable or chicken broth
1 cup full-bodied, dry white wine, such as
　　Chardonnay
1/8 teaspoon freshly ground nutmeg
1 1/2 pounds red potatoes, peeled and
　　finely chopped
8 ounces Cambozola cheese, rind removed,
　　cut into small pieces and softened
Salt and white pepper
2 tablespoons finely chopped
　　chives (optional)

In a large saucepan over medium heat, sauté leek in oil until soft and golden brown. Stir in garlic; cook 2 minutes. Add broth, wine, nutmeg and potatoes; bring to a boil. Reduce heat; cover and simmer 15 minutes, or until potatoes are fork-tender. Add Cambozola; cook, stirring constantly, until cheese melts (don't worry about any blue veins that don't melt).

Pour soup in 2 batches into blender; puree each batch until smooth. To prevent burns, cover blender and begin blending at low speed, gradually increasing to high. If planning to serve cold, pour soup through a medium-fine strainer into a large bowl. Cover and refrigerate for at least 4 hours, or until very cold. Season to taste with salt and pepper. Soup may be refrigerated up to 3 days. If serving hot, return bisque to pan after pureeing; salt and pepper to taste. Keep warm over low heat, but don't let it boil. If desired, sprinkle each serving lightly with chives.

Potatoes

Spud Chili

This potato-pinto bean mélange has become my favorite meatless chili. A simple fact of life is that the success of any chili is greatly dependent on the quality and flavor of the chili powder, of which there are myriad kinds, ranging from light and ultramild, to rich, dark and caramelized, to mouth-searingly hot. Special chili powders are primarily available at gourmet markets and by mail order (for example, Pendery's in Dallas, Texas—1-800-533-1870).

If you haven't the time to soak and cook the beans, you can substitute 4 cups of canned pintos (very well drained), stirring them into the chili during the last 10 minutes of cooking time. Sweet red bell peppers make a colorful substitute for the green bells. Pass bowls of minced jalapeños and sour cream so diners can adjust the heat quotient according to personal taste.

Serves 6

1½ cups dried pinto beans

2 tablespoons olive oil

1 large onion, finely chopped

3 medium cloves garlic, minced

1 medium jalapeño pepper, stemmed, seeded and minced

1 tablespoon good-quality chili powder

1 teaspoon ground cumin

1 teaspoon ground allspice

1 tablespoon chopped, fresh basil or 1 teaspoon dried basil

1½ teaspoons fresh, chopped oregano or ½ teaspoon dried leaf oregano

2 (14½-ounce) cans ready-cut peeled tomatoes and their juice

3 cups vegetable, chicken or beef broth

1½ pounds russet potatoes, well scrubbed and diced

1 medium green bell pepper, cored, seeded and finely chopped

Salt and cayenne pepper

Soak beans overnight in cold water. *Or* use the quick-soak method: Place beans in a large pot; cover with hot water. Bring to a boil; cook 1 minute at high heat. Remove from heat; cover and let stand 1 hour. With either method, drain soaking water from the beans; cover with fresh water 2 inches above the surface of beans. Bring to a boil. Reduce heat and simmer, covered, just until tender, 30 to 40 minutes.

While beans are cooking, heat oil in a large pot. Cook onion over high heat, stirring often, until well browned. Add garlic, jalapeño, chili powder, cumin, allspice, basil and oregano; sauté, stirring often, for 2 minutes. Add tomatoes and their juice and broth, stirring to loosen any bits of browned food clinging to the bottom of pan; bring to a boil. Add potatoes and green pepper; bring to a boil. Cook, uncovered, over medium-high heat for 10 minutes, stirring occasionally. Drain cooked beans and add to chili; cook 10 more minutes, stirring occasionally. Salt and pepper to taste. Chili can be cooled, covered and refrigerated overnight, if desired. Reheat and serve.

Next to jazz music, there is nothing that lifts the spirit and strengthens the soul more than a good bowl of chili.

—Harry James

Roasted Curried Cream Potatoes

You'll note that my restraint in using cream in this book's recipes has been admirable. This recipe, however, is the exception—and rightfully so. The richness of the cream softens the bite of the spicy homemade curry, and the end result is heavenly. Serve this creamy mélange with simply grilled meat or fish, accompanied by a salad of crisp mixed greens tossed with chopped mint and thinly sliced cucumbers.

Serves 4 to 6

1 tablespoon minced fresh ginger

1 large clove garlic, minced

1 teaspoon ground coriander

³/₄ teaspoon salt

³/₄ teaspoon ground cumin

¹/₂ teaspoon ground turmeric

¹/₂ teaspoon ground cinnamon

¹/₂ teaspoon ground cardamom

¹/₄ teaspoon ground nutmeg

¹/₄ teaspoon ground cloves

¹/₈ teaspoon cayenne pepper

1¹/₂ cups heavy cream

2 pounds unpeeled round red or white potatoes, cut into ¹/₄-inch dice

¹/₃ cup chopped scallions (green portion only) or chives

2 tablespoons finely chopped cilantro or mint

Preheat oven to 375°F. Lightly oil a 2-quart gratin dish or other shallow oven-proof dish. In a large bowl, combine ginger, garlic, coriander, salt, cumin, turmeric, cinnamon, cardamom, nutmeg, cloves and cayenne. Slowly stir in cream, mixing until thoroughly combined. Add potatoes; toss to thoroughly coat with cream. Turn mixture into prepared pan. Bake, uncovered, for 15 minutes. Stir well, turning potatoes top to bottom; return to oven for 15 more minutes. Add scallions or chives, stirring to mix in thoroughly. Continue to bake for 15 minutes, or until potatoes are very tender. Garnish by sprinkling with cilantro or mint.

Potato-Chive Focaccia

Focaccia (pronounced foh-KAH-chee-ah) is like a pizza with the topping ingredients kneaded into the dough. This version—which combines mashed potatoes with crispy potato bits—is decidedly moist and tender. For additional potato flavor, use the water in which you boil the potatoes—cooling it first, of course, until it's no hotter than 110°F. Focaccia is great for snacks, to accompany soups or salads, or split horizontally for sandwiches, like the Meatball Muffuletta, page 37.

Serves 8 to 10

1 pound russet potatoes

1 (1/4-ounce) package active dry or quick-rising yeast

1/2 teaspoon granulated sugar

3/4 cup warm (110°F) water

2 3/4–3 1/4 cups bread flour or all-purpose flour

1/4 cup plus about 2 tablespoons olive oil

1/4 cup chopped chives

1 teaspoon salt

1/2 to 1 teaspoon freshly ground black pepper

1 tablespoon coarse-ground polenta or regular yellow cornmeal

1/3 cup grated aged Asiago cheese (about 1 1/2 ounces)

Preheat oven to 400°F. Lightly oil a large baking sheet. Thoroughly scrub, then peel potatoes; reserve skin. Cut 1/2 pound of the potatoes into 1-inch chunks. In a medium saucepan, cook potato chunks in boiling water to cover until fork-tender, about 10 minutes. Drain boiled potatoes immediately and thoroughly. While potatoes are boiling, coarsely grate remaining 1/2 pound raw potatoes; cut reserved potato skins into narrow (about 1/8-inch-wide) strips. Sprinkle grated potatoes and skins in a single layer over prepared baking sheet. Bake for about 20 minutes, tossing every 5 minutes, until potatoes and skins are browned and crispy. Cool to room temperature; crumble finely.

In a 1-cup glass measure, dissolve

yeast and 1 teaspoon of the sugar in warm water. Let stand until foamy, 5 to 10 minutes.

Electric mixer or manual method: Turn boiled potatoes into the large bowl of electric mixer (or any large bowl, if kneading manually). Use a fork to mash potatoes; cool until slightly warm, about 5 minutes. Add yeast mixture, 1 cup of the flour and ¼ cup oil. Use electric mixer fitted with beater(s) to beat at medium speed for 2 minutes (or beat 200 strokes by hand). Add chives, salt and pepper; beat 1 more minute. Change to mixer dough hook(s), or turn dough out onto a lightly floured surface. Add 1½ cups flour and all but ½ cup crumbled crisp potatoes; knead dough by machine or by hand for 6 to 8 minutes, or until smooth and elastic. Add only enough remaining flour to keep dough from being very sticky (it should, however, be quite tacky to the touch). Form dough into ball.

Food processor method: Place boiled potatoes in a workbowl fitted with the plastic kneading blade; process in quick ON/OFF pulses just until potatoes are broken up into small pieces. Add yeast mixture, 1 cup of the flour and ¼ cup oil; process 1 minute. Scrape down sides of bowl; add chives, salt, pepper and 1½ cups flour; process 1 minute. Stop machine; redistribute dough; add all but ½

cup crumbled crisp potatoes. Process 1 more minute. Dough should be elastic, but not sticky. If it is sticky, add a small amount of additional flour. Process 30 seconds, or until flour is incorporated. Turn dough out onto a lightly floured work surface; knead about 1 minute, or until smooth and elastic. Form dough into a ball.

Both methods: Lightly oil a large bowl and place dough in it. Cover bowl with a slightly damp cloth; set in a warm, draft-free place. Let rise until doubled in bulk, about 40 minutes (about 25 minutes with quick-rising yeast).

Generously oil a 9 × 13-inch baking pan; sprinkle bottom evenly with cornmeal. Punch dough down (lightly oiling your hands makes dough easier to handle). Press dough evenly over bottom of prepared pan. Sprinkle with cheese and reserved crumbled crisp potatoes; use your fingertips to press cheese and potatoes firmly into dough's surface. Cover pan with plastic wrap and set in a warm, draft-free place to rise until *almost* doubled in bulk, about 30 minutes (15 minutes with quick-rising yeast).

About 15 minutes before dough is due to be ready, preheat oven to 450°F. Bake 15 to 20 minutes, or until deep golden brown. Remove from oven; cool on a rack about 10 minutes, and cut into 8 to 10 pieces. Serve warm or room temperature.

Yeast Mystique

Yeast is a living organism but it's not at all mysterious. Don't let it intimidate you. All it needs is a little care—don't expose it, or the dough it's in, to extremes of hot and cold or to drafts. Proofing the yeast by combining it with a little sugar and warm liquid ensures that it's still active (it bubbles). If the yeast is dead it won't rise your bread. Just be sure the liquid is in the range of 105° to 115°F. Hot temperatures will kill the yeast and your bread won't rise.

Quick-rising yeast has been specially formulated to leaven (rise) the dough in a third to half the time of regular yeast. The only downside is that accelerated doughs don't produce breads with quite as much flavor as those that are slowly leavened. The bottom line, however, is that no matter how bread is leavened, a homemade loaf nourishes the soul as few storebought versions can.

Cozy Warm Places to Rise Dough

■ Set the bowl of dough on top of the refrigerator (providing it doesn't vibrate).

■ Fill a large bowl with hot water. Position a rack over the bowl of water and set the dough on the rack. Replace water as it cools.

■ Place a pan of hot water on the bottom shelf of a closed oven, with the dough on the shelf above it.

■ Place dough in a gas oven warmed only by the pilot light (tape a note on the oven door to remind yourself there's dough inside).

■ Turn an electric oven on to 200°F for 1 minute, then turn it off.

■ Place dough in a laundry room that's warm and humid from washing clothes (but don't set dough on top of machines that are running).

■ Turn the clothes dryer on the heat cycle for 1 minute; turn off the dryer and put the dough inside.

■ Fill a 2-cup measure with water and bring to a boil in your microwave oven. Push hot water to a back corner of the oven; set dough inside and close the door.

■ Place dough near, but not on, a radiator or heat outlet.

Cheese-Kissed Potato Fans

Cut so that they fan open during baking, these easy and delicious little potatoes are potato-chip crisp on the edges and moist and tender in the middle. Crumbled blue cheese makes a nice substitution for the Parmesan. If the potatoes are super small, you may want to allow 2 per serving for hearty appetites.

Serves 4

3 tablespoons olive oil

1 clove garlic, crushed

4 small (4-ounce) russet potatoes, well scrubbed and dried

Salt and freshly ground black pepper

About 4 tablespoons grated Parmesan or Asiago cheese

Preheat oven to 450°F. In a small bowl, combine oil and garlic; set aside. Place 1 potato in the bowl of a wooden spoon large enough to hold it. Using a sharp knife, and starting 1/4 inch from the end, make cuts at 1/8-inch intervals across potato. The curve of the wooden spoon will prevent the knife from cutting all the way through the potato. Once a potato is cut, gently bend it backward to slightly open the slices. Repeat with remaining potatoes. Place cut potatoes on a large baking sheet, spaced well apart. Brush all over with garlic oil, separating some of the slices to brush the oil inside. Salt and pepper to taste. Bake 45 minutes. Remove from oven. Brush again with oil; sprinkle with cheese. Bake an additional 15 minutes. Serve hot.

The Spice of Life

Because ground spices lose flavor and aroma relatively quickly, buy them in small quantities. Store them airtight in a cool, dark place—never over the stovetop! Spices and spice blends (like chili or curry powder) that will be kept for longer than 6 months should be stored in the refrigerator as soon as they're purchased.

Feisty Oven "Fries"

These potatoes aren't really fried at all, but deliver all the satisfaction of those greasy things with quadruple the calories. The crispy surface is created by a sassy cornstarch slurry. Be selective about the hot sauce you use. There are dozens on the market and they vary widely in flavor. If you're not an aficionado of spicy food, substitute chicken broth for some of the hot sauce. To take the calorie count to its lowest count, use nonfat chicken broth or even water. These "fries" will brown faster if you use two ovens at once, baking on the lowest shelf, which is hotter.

Serves 4

¼ cup cornstarch

2 tablespoons hot pepper sauce

2 tablespoons chicken broth

3 large (about 12-ounce) unpeeled potatoes
(a total of about 2¼ pounds),
scrubbed and well dried

Salt

Arrange oven shelves so one is at the bottom, the other at the top. Preheat oven to 450°F. Generously coat 2 large baking sheets with nonstick vegetable spray (make 3 passes); set aside.

In a small bowl, combine cornstarch and hot pepper sauce until smooth. Gradually stir in chicken broth. Turn the mixture into a large, flat-bottomed dish, spreading across bottom. Cut potatoes into long ½-inch-thick sticks (slice lengthwise and then crosswise at ½-inch intervals). Place potato sticks, a few at a time, in liquid, turning to coat all sides. Place about ½ inch apart on prepared baking sheets. Salt to taste. Bake 20 minutes. Remove from oven; use a metal spatula to flip potatoes. Return to oven, switching position of baking sheets so that the one that was on the top shelf is now on the bottom shelf. Bake 15 to 20 minutes, or until golden brown. Serve hot.

Fabulous French Fries

Before You Start

■ Russets are the best potatoes for frying, although long whites and Yukon golds also work well.

■ Allow 1 medium potato per person.

■ Whether or not you peel the potatoes is up to you. However, French fries with peels have more flavor. If you leave the peels on, scrub the potatoes well.

■ After cutting potatoes into ¼- to ½-inch-thick lengthwise strips, rinse them well in cold water to remove excess starch.

■ Use paper towels to thoroughly dry the potatoes. Any trace of water will cause the oil to boil up violently.

■ To allow for bubbling up and splattering, the pot you use should be filled no more than halfway with oil.

■ The best frying oils are canola, corn, peanut and safflower.

■ The temperature of the oil is all-important and can mean the difference between success and disaster. If the fat isn't hot enough, the potatoes will absorb the oil and be greasy; too hot, and they'll burn.

■ The best way to test the oil temperature is to use a deep-fry thermometer. For an accurate reading, make sure the thermometer's bulb is completely immersed in the oil, but not touching the bottom of the pan.

■ Before beginning to fry potatoes, line one or two baking sheets with a double layer of paper towels on which to drain them.

Let the Frying Begin

■ Drop about a third of the potatoes at a time into 375°F oil. Adding too many potatoes at once will lower the oil's temperature, causing the potatoes to absorb excess oil and become greasy. Fry potatoes until they are golden brown, transfer to paper towel–lined baking sheets to drain. Best served immediately.

■ The classic French method of frying the potatoes twice is more labor-intensive but produces the crispest results. Fry the potatoes first in 325°F oil for 3 to 5 minutes, depending on thickness, or until golden. Drain on paper towels. Once cool, cover and let stand at room temperature up to 4 hours. Just before serving, heat oil to 375°F. Fry potatoes in batches for 1 to 2 minutes or just until golden brown. Drain well and serve immediately.

■ A third French-frying method is to boil the potatoes first. Drop potato sticks into boiling water to cover. Return the water to a soft, rolling boil and cook just until barely fork-tender, 10 to 15 minutes. Use a slotted spoon to transfer potatoes from water to paper towels to drain thoroughly. *Be sure to blot off all excess moisture.* Potatoes may be covered and kept at room temperature up to 4 hours. Fry in 375°F oil until golden brown.

■ Keep each batch of fried potatoes warm in a 275°F oven while you cook the rest.

■ Always return oil to the proper temperature between batches.

■ Season French fries with salt (and pepper, if desired) as soon as you put them on the baking sheet to drain.

■ After cooling the oil completely, remove any food particles by straining oil through a coffee filter, a sieve or a funnel lined with a double layer of cheesecloth. Cover, tightly seal and refrigerate oil for reuse.

Food for Thought
■ Ounce for ounce, French fries contain 12 times the fat and almost 3 times the calories of a baked potato.

'Tis unwise to joke about marriage or potatoes.

—old Irish saying

Tips on Grating Cheese

■ Hard cheeses like Parmesan and Asiago are easier to grate at room temperature, whereas semifirm cheeses like cheddar and Swiss are more easily grated when cold.

■ When using the food processor to chop (rather than shred) cheese, cut cheese into 1-inch chunks—larger pieces can jam the metal blade.

■ To grate hard cheeses like Parmesan in a food processor, use the metal blade rather than the grating disk. With the machine running, drop small (1 inch) chunks of cheese into the processor workbowl, waiting until 1 chunk is grated before adding another.

■ Speed cleanup by spraying nonstick vegetable spray on a food processor's grating disk or metal blade so the cheese won't stick. When working with soft cheeses like Muenster (which tends to make a mess), also spray the inside of the processor workbowl and cover.

■ *Cheese yields:* Four ounces ($1/4$ pound) hard, semifirm or semisoft cheese = about 1 cup grated cheese.

*Just give me a potato, any kind of potato,
and I'm happy.*

—Dolly Parton

Potato-Garlic Roast

This easy, eminently satisfying dish delivers crisp, browned potatoes and creamy-soft garlic; the latter can be squeezed out of its skin and spread on the potatoes. A food processor fitted with the 3mm slicing blade makes quick work of slicing the potatoes, which I don't peel because I like the flavor of the skins.

Serves 6

2 pounds russet potatoes, scrubbed and cut crosswise into $1/8$-inch slices

1 cup beef broth

1 tablespoon minced fresh rosemary or 1 teaspoon dried rosemary

1 large head garlic, broken into cloves but unpeeled

Salt and freshly ground black pepper

1 tablespoon olive oil

4 ounces fontina, Cambozola, Gouda or other cheese, finely chopped (optional)

Preheat oven to 350°F. Generously oil a 9 × 13-inch baking pan or dish. Evenly layer half of the potatoes over bottom of pan. Drizzle with $1/2$ cup beef broth, sprinkle with half the rosemary; salt and pepper to taste. Repeat with remaining potatoes, remaining $1/2$ cup beef broth, rosemary, salt and pepper to taste. Tuck garlic cloves randomly amid potatoes. Bake 1 hour.

Increase oven heat to 400°F. Brush olive oil over potatoes. Bake 30 minutes more, or until potatoes are brown and crispy. If desired, sprinkle cheese over potatoes 10 minutes before end of baking time.

Peace of mind and a comfortable income are predicted by a dream of eating potatoes in any form.

—Ned Ballantyne and Stella Coeli
Your Horoscope and Dreams

Mint Pesto Roasted Potatoes

This versatile dish is absolutely wonderful in the summer when mint is abundant. Serve it hot, at room temperature or as a salad (*see* following variation). Although mint particularly complements new potatoes, you can vary the pesto according to your personal whimsy. For instance, you can substitute basil, arugula or watercress for the mint; or pine nuts, walnuts or pistachios for the almonds.

Serves 4 to 6

Potatoes

¹/₃ cup olive or canola oil

2 pounds tiny new potatoes, cut in half

Salt and freshly ground black pepper

3 medium cloves garlic, unpeeled

Mint Pesto

2 cups firmly packed mint leaves

¹/₂ cup well-toasted slivered almonds

1 cup olive oil

2 tablespoons lemon or lime juice

¹/₃ cup grated Parmesan or aged Asiago cheese

Potatoes

Preheat oven to 375°F. Pour oil into a large baking pan with shallow sides (a 17 × 11-inch jelly-roll pan works well). Add potatoes, turning to coat all sides with oil; salt and pepper to taste. Scatter garlic cloves randomly amid potatoes. Potatoes will roast better if there's a little space between them. Bake 20 minutes. Remove garlic cloves; set aside. Flip potatoes to brown other side; bake additional 15 to 20 minutes, or until potatoes are fork-tender.

Mint Pesto

Meanwhile, squeeze the 3 cloves of roasted garlic out of their skins into a food processor fitted with the metal chopping blade. Add mint and almonds; process until pureed, scraping down sides of workbowl as necessary. With machine running, slowly add oil, processing until mixture is smooth. Add cheese and lemon or lime juice; process to blend. Salt and pepper to taste.

In a large bowl, toss pesto with hot roasted potatoes; serve immediately.

■ **Mint Pesto Roasted Potato Salad:**
After tossing pesto and roasted potatoes together, bring to room temperature. Add 2 large, seeded and coarsely chopped tomatoes and ½ cup Niçoise olives; toss to coat with pesto. Serve at room temperature or very slightly chilled.

What small potatoes we are, compared with what we might be.
We don't plow deep enough, any of us, for one thing.

—Charles Dudley, *My Summer in a Garden*

Perfect Roasted Potatoes

■   Any potato can be roasted. Although long whites, round reds and whites and new potatoes are considered best, don't turn up your nose at the versatile russet.

■   To prepare potatoes for roasting, halve the small to medium ones (leave tiny new potatoes whole); cut larger specimens into quarters, sixths or eighths. Pour ¼ to ⅓ cup olive oil, a combination of oil and melted butter, pan drippings or melted lard into a shallow baking dish or pan. Add potatoes and toss to liberally coat with fat. Salt and pepper to taste, and roast in a preheated 375°F oven for 1 to 1½ hours, or until crisp and brown on the outside and fork-tender.

■   The secret of perfectly roasted potatoes is to turn them every 10 to 15 minutes so they get evenly crisp and brown.

■   Serve roasted potatoes hot from the oven—leftovers somehow never regain that crispy texture.

■   Leftover roasted potatoes make excellent potato salad. Simply cut them into bite-size pieces and combine with the dressing of your choice.

The Perfect Baked Potato

"My idea of heaven is a great big baked potato and someone to share it with."

—Oprah Winfrey

First You Buy Them

■ Russet potatoes are the best for baking, a process that transforms their starchy flesh into a light and fluffy texture.

■ Choose potatoes that are the same size so they'll get done at the same time. A 6- to 8-ounce potato is about 1 serving.

■ Scrub potatoes under running water; blot dry with paper towels. Prick them about 1 inch deep in several places with the tines of a fork so steam can escape during baking.

■ For a crisper, browner skin, rub a little olive or vegetable oil, butter or bacon fat all over the potato's surface. Oiled potatoes also bake slightly faster.

■ Don't wrap potatoes in foil unless you want steamed potatoes with flaccid skins.

■ If you want to bake a lot of potatoes at one time, stand them on end in a 12-cup muffin tin.

Then You Bake Them

■ Potatoes can be baked at temperatures from 350° to 450°F, and will take anywhere from 45 minutes to about $1\frac{1}{4}$ hours to cook, depending on the potato's size and the oven's temperature. Higher temperatures deliver the crispest skin.

■ Bake potatoes right on the oven rack so air can circulate around them.

■ Cut a potato's baking time by almost a third by skewering it with an aluminum potato nail (do not do this in a microwave oven), available at gourmet shops.

■ It's sad but true that microwaved "baked" potatoes just can't live up to their oven-baked counterparts. If you're in a hurry, however, put the fork-pierced potatoes in a microwave oven; cook at HIGH (100 percent power) for 3 minutes for 1 potato, 4 minutes for 2 potatoes, 5 minutes for 3 potatoes, etc. Remove potatoes from microwave oven and immediately place in a preheated 450°F oven for 20 to 25 minutes.

■ If you're in a real hurry, you can completely cook potatoes in a microwave oven (though they certainly won't have the same flesh or skin texture as baked potatoes). Pierce 6- to 8-ounce potatoes with a fork and cook at HIGH for: 1 potato, 4 to 6 minutes; 2 potatoes, 6 to 8 minutes; 3 potatoes, 8 to 10 minutes; 4 potatoes, 10 to 12 minutes, and so forth. (These are approximate cooking times and will depend on the size of the potatoes and the wattage of the oven.) Let potatoes stand for 5 minutes in the microwave oven before serving.

■ To test potatoes for doneness, insert the tines of a fork deep into their flesh—there should be no resistance.

Tempting Toppings

■ To serve a baked potato, use a sharp knife to slit it down the center; squeeze both ends together to open the potato and expose the flesh.

■ *Watching calories?* Use low-fat sour cream instead of regular sour cream (the non-fat variety is gelatinous and tastes nasty). *Or* combine cottage cheese and a little milk in the blender, and process until smooth; season to taste with salt and pepper. *Or* try Quark, a soft, low-calorie cheese (low-fat or nonfat) with a flavor that's similar to sour cream and a texture richer than either low-fat sour cream or yogurt. *Or* mix ¼ cup salsa with ½ cup low-fat sour cream to top your potato.

■ Chopped herbs (basil, chives, dill or watercress); crumbled crisp bacon; sautéed onions; roasted garlic blended with sour cream or Quark or butter; grated cheese (cheddar, fontina, Monterey Jack, Parmesan or Swiss) or crumbled feta or blue cheese; toasted caraway, celery, fennel, poppy or sesame seeds; curry or chili powder; cayenne pepper or freshly ground black pepper; diced red or green bell peppers, jalapeños or other chiles, scallions or seeded tomatoes; a mélange of chopped olives, or Dickie Brennan's Olive Salad, page 38; or caviar. Combine sour cream, Quark, or cottage cheese with any of these toppings.

■ Make a meal by topping a baked potato with chili.

Baked Potato Encores

■ Wrap cooled leftover *whole* baked potatoes and refrigerate up to 3 days. To reheat, soak potato in hot water for 1 minute, then bake at 350°F for about 20 minutes.

■ Leftover whole baked potatoes can be frozen (after cooling) up to 3 months by wrapping in heavy-duty foil, then in a plastic bag. Thaw overnight in the fridge, then unwrap and bake potatoes at 350°F for 30 minutes. *Or* bake frozen, foil-wrapped potatoes at 350°F for about 45 minutes, removing foil for the final 15 minutes of baking time.

■ Cut leftover baked potatoes into ½-inch pieces and toss with a little olive oil. Sauté over high heat, tossing often, for 10 to 15 minutes, or until crisp and brown. *Or* bake uncovered at 425°F, turning occasionally, until crisp and golden brown, 30 to 45 minutes. Season to taste with salt and freshly ground black pepper, or season with chili powder, cayenne pepper or minced fresh herbs.

■ Cut leftovers into ½-inch pieces and sauté with other vegetables, corned beef, etc., for hash.

■ *Crispy potato skins:* Don't throw out leftover baked potato skins—scrape out the flesh and brush the skins with olive oil. Use scissors to cut the skins into ½-inch-wide strips, then sprinkle with salt, pepper and, if desired, a little chili powder. Bake at 400°F until crispy (about 10 minutes). These crispy strips are great for snacks and appetizers, or crumble them and use as a garnish for soups and salads.

Hot Smoked Potatoes

These smoke-infused morsels are perfect companions for hearty meats like sausages or ribs. Use almost any kind of potato—Yukon golds, butterballs, round reds, long whites or russets. Try briefly smoking cooked russet halves to create amazing mashed potatoes! Or use leftover smoked potatoes for an unforgettable potato salad or hash. One caveat: Oversmoking the potatoes will completely overwhelm their potato-y flavor, so here subtlety is the byword.

Serves 4 to 6

2 pounds potatoes (any variety), unpeeled

1/2 cup olive oil

2 medium cloves garlic, minced

2 tablespoons finely chopped fresh
  rosemary, basil or cilantro

Salt and freshly ground black pepper

Scrub potatoes well under running water; cut into chunks about 1 inch square. Cook potatoes in a large pot of boiling water for 5 minutes, or just until *barely* fork-tender. While potatoes are cooking, combine oil, garlic and herbs in the jar of an electric blender. Cover and process on high for 30 to 60 seconds, or until well combined. Pour into a 9 × 13-inch pan. Add drained hot potatoes; toss to thoroughly coat with herbed oil. Cover and set aside at room temperature for 2 hours, or refrigerate overnight.

At least 1 hour before smoking the potatoes, soak 2 cups wood chips in water to cover. When ready, light fire in outdoor grill according to manufacturer's directions. Just before beginning to grill, sprinkle drained wood chips over heat source; adjust upper and lower grill vents so they're open only a quarter of the way. Place potatoes on the grill; cover and cook 3 minutes. Use tongs to turn potatoes. Grill, uncovered, 5 more minutes, or until potatoes are fork-tender. Serve hot.

Where There's Fire There's Smoke

Wood smoke adds flavorful nuances to grilled foods. The only woods that should be used for cooking are fruitwoods (apple, cherry and peach) or hardwoods (alder, hickory, maple, mesquite and oak). Never under any circumstances use softwoods (pine and spruce), which exude noxious resins and fumes. Both wood chips and wood chunks are marketed today. The chips cook faster and also take less soaking time, a necessary procedure so the wood doesn't go up in flames shortly after it goes on the heat source.

Options to wood chips include grapevines (available by mail order unless you live near a vineyard), herbs and nuts (crack whole walnuts or pecans)—all of which should be soaked for 1 hour before being tossed on the coals. Other flavorings can be used in conjunction with wood chips— orange peels or whole garlic cloves or nutmegs, for example. Bottom line: Any flavoring should complement the food being grilled. And it goes without saying that one should always follow the grill manufacturer's instructions before using wood for grilling.

'Tis the potato that's the queen of the garden.

—Irish saying

Mashed Potato Mix-ins

In his book *Love After Lunch*, Andrew Payne wrote: "Mashed potato is the gentile's chicken noodle soup. It's nature's tranquilizer, I take it instead of Valium."

I couldn't agree more. I like my mashed potatoes smooth, but with a twist. Just before serving, I fold in "mix-ins" such as finely chopped watercress or tomatoes, crispy crumbled bacon, or crunchy sunflower seeds. The mix-ins not only contribute color and texture, but add so much flavor that the temptation to gild the lily with butter and cream is greatly reduced. Most of the following mix-ins (see page 83) don't require cooking—the heat of the freshly mashed potatoes "cooks" them slightly. The following basic mashed potato recipe employs olive oil (and not much at that) instead of butter to reduce saturated fat. If you're absolutely in the mood for sin, however, this amount of potatoes will easily absorb 2 sticks of butter, melted.

Serves 4

Basic Mashed Potatoes

2 pounds russet or Yukon gold (or your favorite) potatoes
1–2 tablespoons olive oil
$^1/_2$–$^3/_4$ cup warm liquid (milk, cream, chicken broth, potato water)
$^1/_2$–$1^1/_2$ cups Mix-ins (page 83) (optional)
Salt and freshly ground black pepper

Scrub potatoes well under running water; cut into 1-inch pieces. (Potatoes can be peeled first—save peels to broil until crisp and use as mix-ins, if desired.) In a large saucepan, bring water (enough to cover potatoes) to a boil. Add potatoes; cook 15 to 20 minutes, or just until fork-tender. Drain thoroughly; peel potatoes if desired. *Or* place potatoes in a steamer basket and set over boiling water. Steam just until tender. Return potatoes to empty pan; cook over low heat, shaking pan often, for about 1 minute, or until excess moisture evaporates.

Press hot potatoes through a potato ricer or a sieve with large holes into a large, preferably heated bowl. *Or* turn hot potatoes into a bowl and mash with a large fork or potato masher. Then, with a wire whisk lightly beat potatoes, adding oil and enough liquid to reach desired smooth consistency. If desired, add mix-ins, folding to combine; salt and pepper to taste.

■ **Smoked Mashed Potatoes:** Bake whole russets in a 350°F oven for about 1 hour, or until fork-tender. Cut potatoes in half lengthwise; brush cut sides with olive oil. Over a charcoal fire with soaked wood chips (see page 81), place potatoes, cut side down, on grill. Adjust upper and lower grill vents so they're only open a quarter of the way. Cover and cook 3 to 5 minutes, depending on the amount of smoke flavor desired. Scoop pulp out of skins and mash.

Mix-ins

- finely chopped watercress, parsley or arugula
- finely shredded fresh spinach leaves
- crumbled crisp bacon
- finely chopped herbs, such as basil, chives, cilantro, dill, mint or tarragon
- chopped seeded tomatoes
- minced sun-dried tomatoes
- minced red or green bell pepper (or some of each)
- grated cheese, such as fontina, Gruyère or cheddar
- soft-ripened cheese (such as Cambozola or Brie), rind removed, cut into small pieces
- finely diced tart apple, either raw or briefly sautéed
- toasted sunflower seeds
- minced jalapeños or other chiles (go easy!—start with 2 tablespoons)

- mushrooms (about ⅓ pound), finely chopped and sautéed until browned
- chopped imported olives, black or green
- crumbled crisp potato skins (toast them under the broiler)
- finely chopped red onion, sautéed until soft
- 6 to 8 cloves roasted garlic, squeezed out of the skins and mashed until smooth
- 1 to 2 tablespoons tomato paste (whip in with liquid) and scallions
- tomato, ham or bacon and scallions
- watercress, plus apples and cheddar
- onions and apples
- roasted garlic and cheese
- mushrooms and spinach
- Greek olives and feta cheese
- watercress, tomato and onions
- sunflower seeds and apples

Tips for Great Mashed Potatoes

Almost *any* potato can be used for mashing—starchy specimens like russets produce the lightest, fluffiest results, while waxier potatoes like butterballs and Yukon golds are creamy-smooth.

Cooking the Potatoes

■ The best way to cook potatoes for mashing is either boiling or steaming, though baked potatoes can also be mashed. Microwaving potatoes for mashing isn't recommended.

■ Scrub the potatoes well before cooking them in their skins, which not only retains nutrients but also flavors the water, which you can use to moisten the mashed potatoes.

■ The smaller you cut the potatoes, the faster they'll cook.

■ If you love potato skins mixed into mashed potatoes, cut the potatoes into small cubes *before* cooking—the end result will be tiny bits of potato skin flavoring the mix rather than large unappealing chunks.

■ Or invest a little extra effort by peeling the potatoes before cooking, broiling the skins until crisp while the potatoes are cooking, then folding the crumbled, crisp potato skins into the mashed potatoes just before serving.

■ For subtly smoky mashed potatoes, add a ham hock or smoked sausage link (split lengthwise) to the cold cooking water; bring water to a boil and cook for 5 minutes before adding potatoes. Before draining and mashing potatoes, remove ham hock or sausage and reserve for another use.

■ For extra-rich mashed potatoes, cook the potatoes in milk or in half milk, half water. Save the liquid to use for soups or sauces.

■ Cook the potatoes only until fork-tender; drain immediately so they don't absorb excess moisture. After draining the potatoes, return them to the pan and cook over low heat for about 1 minute, shaking the pan often, to evaporate excess moisture and steam.

Doing the Mash

■ The amount of liquid to be added to mashed potatoes depends on the type of potato—drier potatoes like russets require more liquid than higher-moisture specimens.

■ The liquid added to mashed potatoes will affect both flavor and texture. Cream and sour cream add richness and body, while non- or low-fat milk produces light, fluffy potatoes. The water in which the potatoes were cooked not only delivers a flavor bonus but is fat-free. For wonderful flavor, use a couple of tablespoons of white wine as part of the liquid.

■ Though it's preferable to add hot (or at least warm) liquid to mashed potatoes it isn't absolutely necessary. If you use cold milk, add it very slowly, whipping constantly, so you won't end up with glue.

■ To mash potatoes, use a potato ricer, potato masher or a large fork—an electric mixer can cause potatoes to become sticky, while food processors make glue.

■ For ultimate decadence, whip ½ cup heavy cream until stiff and fold into mashed potatoes just before serving.

■ Serve mashed potatoes in a heated bowl to keep them at their peak longer.

■ Mashed potatoes are decidedly best served immediately. If it's necessary to hold them, however, brush the surface with melted butter; cover and keep warm in a 250°F oven for no more than 30 minutes. Or reheat in a microwave oven by covering and cook them at HIGH (*100 percent power*) for 1 to 2 minutes, depending on the amount. Stir potatoes before serving.

■ If you're going to hold mashed potatoes, don't stir in any mix-ins until just before serving.

Using Leftovers

■ Mix cold mashed potatoes with ground meat (replace up to one third of the meat) for moist, lower-fat hamburger patties.

■ Form leftover mashed potatoes into patties, dip in beaten egg, then into bread crumbs. Let dry in the refrigerator for 1 hour before frying until crisp and golden brown on both sides.

■ Use leftover mashed potatoes as a thickener for soups, stews and sauces.

■ Combine with chopped, sautéed vegetables and use to stuff bell peppers (see page 90).

Bourbon-Smashed Sweets

One of the guiding lights of my early food career was my dear friend the late Bert Greene, an inestimable sage of American food. This recipe was inspired by Bert's "Mashed Sweets" from his 1984 classic, *Greene on Greens,* which was inducted into the Cookbook Hall of Fame in 1995. If you're not a bourbon fan, dark rum makes a splendid substitute. Those who are liquor-sensitive can use orange or apple juice with equally delicious (though decidedly different) results.

Serves 4

2 pounds sweet potatoes, cooked until tender
1/2 teaspoon ground cardamom
1/4 teaspoon freshly ground nutmeg
1/3 cup whipping cream
2 tablespoons bourbon
Salt and freshly ground black pepper

Cut potatoes in half; use a spoon to scrape potato pulp out of skins and into a medium saucepan over low heat. Add cardamom, nutmeg, cream and bourbon; mash with a potato masher until smooth. Heat until warmed through. Salt and pepper to taste.

Spirited Cooking

In the not-too-distant past it was thought that any and all alcohol in potables evaporated when heated, lulling many to believe such dishes were "safe." However, a USDA study has shown that anywhere from 5 to 85 percent alcohol may remain in a cooked dish. The wide range is due to many factors, including how a food is heated (boiled, baked, etc.), the cooking time and the source of the alcohol. So, caution is the byword for alcohol-sensitive people for whom even the slightest trace of alcohol is ill-advised.

Potatoes

Meat and Potatoes

Heaven-and-Earth Pork Pot Pie

The quaint name of this truly comforting dish comes from the age-old duo of apples (heaven) and potatoes (earth). Pork sirloin, which in its cut-up form is sometimes labeled "pork kebabs," can be substituted for the loin; so can pork tenderloin, if you're feeling prosperous. Although I created the Cornmeal Crumble Topping as an easy change of pace from a traditional crust, I've found it's also a great stand-in for croutons in salads and soups.

Serves 6

Cornmeal Crumble Topping

1 cup all-purpose flour

3/4 cup fine yellow cornmeal

2 tablespoons packed brown sugar

1/2 teaspoon salt

1/2 teaspoon ground allspice

1/2 cup (1 stick) cold butter, cut into
8 pieces

3 tablespoons ice water

Filling

4 strips thick-sliced lean smoked bacon

1 1/2 pounds boneless pork loin, trimmed of
excess fat and cut into 3/4-inch chunks

1 1/2 tablespoons sugar

1/4 cup olive oil or reserved bacon
drippings

1 medium onion, finely chopped

1 pound long white or Yukon gold potatoes
(peeling optional), cut into
1/2-inch chunks

2 medium cloves garlic, minced

1 tablespoon minced fresh or seasoned
sliced ginger

1/2 teaspoon freshly ground nutmeg

1/4 cup all-purpose flour

2 cups chicken broth

1 very large (about 9 ounces) tart, crisp
apple (peeling optional), cut into
1/2-inch chunks

Salt and freshly ground black pepper

Cornmeal Crumble Topping

Position oven rack in center of oven; preheat oven to 300°F. Lightly oil a 17 × 11-inch jelly-roll pan or other large baking pan with shallow sides. In a medium bowl or a food processor workbowl fitted with the metal blade, combine the flour, cornmeal, brown sugar, salt and allspice.

By hand: Use a pastry cutter or 2 knives to cut in butter until mixture resembles coarse crumbs.

By food processor: Process dry ingredients 2 seconds. Add butter; process in quick ON/OFF pulses until mixture resembles coarse crumbs.

Both methods: Add ice water; stir with a fork or by machine process (with quick ON/OFF pulses) just until mixture begins to hold together. Crumble mixture evenly onto prepared pan—chunks should be no larger than 3/4 inch in diameter. Bake 15 minutes; use a metal spatula to gently flip mixture, redistributing it evenly. Bake 15 minutes more. Remove from oven; cool in pan until ready to use.

Filling

Preheat oven to 350°F. Lightly oil a shallow, 3-quart casserole (I use a 9 × 7-inch rectangular dish that's 2 inches deep). In a large skillet over medium heat, fry bacon until very crisp. Transfer to paper towels to drain. Crumble bacon when cool; set aside. Pour bacon drippings into a small container and reserve. Add pork to same skillet; sprinkle with sugar. Sauté over medium-high heat, stirring often, until pork is well browned on all sides. Add 1/4 cup olive oil or reserved bacon drippings and onion; cook over medium-high heat for 5 minutes. Add potatoes; cover and cook over medium-low heat for 10 minutes, stirring occasionally. Add garlic, ginger, nutmeg and flour; cook for 2 minutes. Stirring constantly, gradually add chicken broth, loosening any bits of browned food clinging to bottom of pan. Cook until mixture thickens and comes to a boil, 2 to 3 minutes. Remove from heat; stir in apple and crumbled bacon; salt and pepper to taste. Turn mixture into prepared pan; sprinkle evenly with cornmeal crumble. Bake 20 minutes; serve hot.

Mashed Potato–Stuffed Peppers

This immensely satisfying dish can easily become vegetarian by substituting 1 cup parboiled chopped broccoli for the bacon. For a delicious variation, try 1 cup chopped smoked ham instead of bacon. I've given you the dimensions for the peppers because that's the perfect size for the amount of stuffing. Most stuffed-pepper recipes call for parboiling the peppers, but I skip that step. This not only saves time but delivers a firmer pepper. Seeding the tomatoes is important—not doing so makes the stuffing too wet.

Serves 4

4 red or green bell peppers, about 4 inches tall and 3 1/2 inches in diameter
1 1/4 pounds russet potatoes, cooked, cooled and peeled
1 egg, well beaten
1/2 cup sour cream, regular or low-fat
1/4 teaspoon freshly ground nutmeg
1/4 teaspoon salt
Pinch of cayenne pepper

Freshly ground black pepper
1/2 pound thick-sliced lean bacon, fried until crisp, cooled and crumbled
1 medium tomato, seeded and finely chopped
1 cup fresh corn kernels (about 1 medium ear)
2 scallions (green portion only), snipped into 1/4-inch lengths
1 cup shredded sharp cheddar cheese (about 4 ounces)

Preheat oven to 375°F. Cut about 1/2 inch from tops of peppers; remove seeds. Arrange peppers upright in a lightly oiled 8 × 8-inch baking pan. In a large bowl, mash potatoes until smooth. Add egg, sour cream, nutmeg, salt, cayenne and black pepper to taste; stir to combine. Reserve 1/4 cup crumbled bacon. Fold in remaining bacon, tomato, corn, scallions and cheese. Spoon potato mixture into bell pepper cavities; sprinkle tops of stuffing with remaining bacon crumbles. Bake 45 minutes, or until peppers are tender. Serve hot.

Herbed Potato Burgers

Good news for cholesterol watchers: These burgers contain only two thirds the meat and have 100 percent flavor! And you can get away with using lean ground beef because the potatoes add the moistness that would normally be contributed by fat. How finely you grate the potatoes depends on how well done you want the burgers. The regular shredding disk on my food processor produces rather thick shreds that are still *al dente* by the time the burgers are done (I like the contrast in texture). If you prefer your potatoes softer or like burgers medium rare, finely shred the potatoes and shape the patties so they're no more than about 3/8 inch thick—that way the potatoes will be cooked through. Or if you want thicker but well-done potato shreds, lightly sauté the potatoes, cool, then mix them in with the meat.

Serves 6 to 8

2 pounds lean ground beef

1 pound russet or long white potatoes, shredded

2/3 cup packed basil leaves, finely chopped

1/4 cup snipped chives

1/2 teaspoon salt

1/2 teaspoon freshly ground black pepper

In a large bowl, mix all ingredients until well combined. Shape into 6 to 8 (1/2- to 3/4-inch-thick) patties. Broil, fry or grill the burgers until done according to personal preference. If grilling, soak 2 cups wood chips in water to cover at least 1 hour before beginning to cook. When ready, light fire in outdoor grill according to manufacturer's directions. Just before beginning to grill, sprinkle drained wood chips over heat source. For a smokier-flavored burger, cover the grill during cooking.

■ **Hidden Treasure Burgers:** Make a pocket in the center of each hamburger patty. Insert a 1-ounce chunk of cheese; cover completely with meat mixture, securing all openings so cheese doesn't seep out when it melts during cooking. Some of my favorite cheeses include blue cheese, fontina, sharp cheddar, Cambozola and smoked Gouda.

■ **Bacon Burgers:** Add 1 cup crisply cooked, finely crumbled bacon to meat mixture.

■ **Ham Burgers:** Substitute 1 pound ground smoked ham for 1 pound of the ground beef.

A hamburger is warm and fragrant and juicy... soft and nonthreatening....
A hamburger is companionable and faintly erotic.

—Tom Robbins

Burger Tips

■ For general information on buying ground meat, see page 36.

■ When shaping hamburger patties, remember that there's more shrinkage in higher-fat meats than lean meats. So, when using ground chuck or regular ground beef, form the patties slightly larger than the diameter of the hamburger bun—they'll shrink down to just about the right size.

■ Overworking a mixture results in dense, heavy burgers. Mix ingredients only until they are combined; shape the patties quickly.

■ While shaping the patties, dampen your hands with cold water and the meat won't cling to your fingers as much.

■ The way you shape and cook hamburgers is important. Thin, quickly cooked (over high heat) patties produce well-done burgers with lots of crusty (seared) surface. Thick, slowly cooked patties yield succulent and juicy burgers.

■ Preheating the pan produces burgers with a flavorful seared surface.

■ Pressing down on a hamburger patty with a spatula doesn't speed the cooking, but it definitely squeezes out some of the juices.

■ To ensure food safety and guard against bacterial infection, cook burgers until well done.

Sweet 'n' Sassy Potato-Sausage Salad

This recipe, a rendition of one in my book *Cooking Smart,* always gets raves. Yukon gold or yellow Finnish potatoes can be substituted for the new potatoes, and sweet potatoes make a particularly tantalizing stand-in. If you use sweets, be sure to cut them into sixths before boiling and peel them after they're cooked. Cook only until *barely* tender when pierced with the tip of a knife—overcooked sweet potatoes have a tendency to fall apart. If you can't find fresh limes, substitute fresh lemon juice. Don't, I implore you, use bottled lime or lemon juice, which has a slightly synthetic flavor. Use your favorite smoked sausage—I particularly like *lop chong,* a spicy Chinese sausage. Another winner is kielbasa, which is now available in a lower-fat style made with turkey, beef and pork.

Serves 6 to 8

2 pounds small new potatoes, unpeeled and well scrubbed

2 medium cloves garlic, minced

1 tablespoon minced fresh ginger

2 tablespoons granulated sugar

1/2 teaspoon salt

2/3 cup olive or vegetable oil

1/3 cup sour cream

1/4 cup fresh lime juice

2 teaspoons Dijon mustard

3/4 teaspoon chili powder

1/2–3/4 teaspoon cayenne pepper

3/4 pound smoked, fully cooked sausage, diced

6 scallions (green portion only), chopped

3/4 cup chopped jícama

1/2 cup finely chopped red bell pepper

1/2 cup finely chopped watercress

Salt and freshly ground black pepper

In a large pot of boiling water, cook potatoes until tender when pierced with the tip of a knife, about 10 to 20 minutes, depending on the size of the potatoes.

While potatoes are cooking, combine garlic, ginger, sugar and salt in a large bowl. Use the back of a large spoon to mash ingredients together. Add oil, sour cream, lime juice, mustard, chili powder and cayenne, whisking until thoroughly combined.

Drain cooked potatoes thoroughly. Return them to the pan over medium-high heat, shaking pan to toss potatoes until all residual moisture evaporates. Cut hot potatoes into $\frac{1}{2}$-inch chunks; toss with dressing. Add sausage, scallions, jícama, bell peppers and watercress, tossing to combine. Salt and pepper to taste. Cover and refrigerate at least 3 hours before serving. Let stand at room temperature 30 minutes before serving.

The easiest way to chop chives or the green portion of scallions is to snip them with kitchen shears or other scissors.

Greek Osso Buco

This Greek rendition of an Italian classic features mint, which Greeks utilize much as Italians use basil. I also tested this recipe replacing the mint with dill, which gives the dish an entirely different but equally delicious character. Don't forget the bonus that comes with shank bones—the rich marrow, which can be scooped out of the bones and spread on chunks of crusty bread. The only other accompaniment this meal-in-one dish needs is a tomato-cucumber salad sprinkled with feta cheese and capers.

Serves 4 to 6

3 meaty lamb shanks (about 3 pounds), each cut into 3 pieces

1/2 cup flour

Salt and freshly ground black pepper

3 tablespoons olive oil

1 large onion, coarsely chopped

7 large cloves garlic, finely chopped, divided

1 tablespoon ground coriander

1 1/2 cups full-bodied red wine, such as Cabernet Sauvignon or Zinfandel

2 cups hot lamb (or half beef, half chicken) broth

2 (14 1/2-ounce) cans ready-cut peeled tomatoes, with their juice

3 tablespoons finely grated lemon zest (about 2 medium lemons), divided

1 (9-ounce) package frozen artichoke halves, thawed

1 pound round red potatoes (peeling optional), cut into 1-inch chunks

2/3 cup plus 3 tablespoons finely chopped fresh mint

1/4 cup fresh lemon juice

Preheat oven to 350°F. Trim lamb of excess fat. In a medium bowl, combine flour with salt and pepper to taste. Coat lamb pieces with flour mixture, shaking off any excess. Heat oil in a large Dutch oven or skillet with high sides. Over medium-high heat, cook meat until well browned on both sides; transfer to a large plate. In same skillet over medium-high heat, sauté onion, stirring occasionally, until golden brown. Stir in 6 chopped cloves of garlic; sauté 2 minutes. Return lamb and any juices to pan. Add coriander, wine, broth, tomatoes with their juice and 2 tablespoons lemon zest, stirring to scrape up browned bits on bottom of pan. Bring to a boil. Cover and bake in the oven 1¼ hours. Add artichokes, potatoes and ⅓ cup mint.

Cover and bake 30 minutes more, or until potatoes and lamb are fork-tender.

Remove pan from oven. Use a slotted spoon to transfer meat and vegetables to a platter; place in a 250°F oven to keep warm. Don't worry if you leave some of the tomatoes in the pan. Stir in lemon juice; bring mixture to a boil over high heat. Cook, stirring often, until sauce is reduced by a third.

While sauce is reducing, make a mint gremolata by combining remaining 1 chopped clove garlic, 1 tablespoon lemon zest and 3 tablespoons mint in a small bowl. Sprinkle over meat and vegetables. Just before serving, stir in remaining ⅓ cup chopped mint into sauce; serve sauce on the side.

Spiced-Twice Potato Hash

Regular and sweet potatoes make a delicious duo in this easy hash. I prefer the dark-fleshed sweets (see page 53) because they add such a beautiful color, but you can substitute light-fleshed sweet potatoes if you prefer. Cut the apples and potatoes the same size (about ½-inch dice). Smoked ham (about ½ pound, diced) can be substituted for the bacon. In the summer, when fresh corn is abundant, I add 1 cup corn kernels along with the apples.

Makes 6 servings

1 pound thick-sliced lean bacon

2 cups diced tart apples (about 2 medium apples), peeling optional

1 tablespoon fresh lemon juice

2 tablespoons bacon drippings or vegetable oil

1 large onion, finely chopped

2 cups peeled, diced sweet potatoes (about ¾ pound)

2 cups diced russet or all-purpose potatoes (about ¾ pound), peeling optional

½ teaspoon ground nutmeg

½ teaspoon ground allspice

¼ teaspoon ground cinnamon

⅛ teaspoon ground cloves

⅓ cup water

Salt and freshly ground black pepper

In a large skillet over medium-high heat, cook bacon until crisp. While bacon is cooking, toss apples with lemon juice; set aside. Transfer cooked bacon to paper towels to drain. Pour off all but 1 tablespoon bacon drippings (or pour off all bacon drippings and add 1 tablespoon vegetable oil to skillet). Sauté onion over high heat until browned. Add remaining tablespoon bacon drippings or oil, then potatoes; cook over high heat, stirring often, about 7 minutes, or until potatoes are browned. Reduce heat to medium. Stir in nutmeg, allspice, cinnamon, cloves and water; cover and cook just until potatoes are tender, about 5 minutes. While potatoes are cooking, crumble bacon. Stir in apples; cook, uncovered, over medium-high heat for 2 minutes (all liquid should be evaporated). Add crumbled bacon; cook 1 minute. Salt and pepper to taste. Serve immediately.

The Nuances of Nutmeg

Freshly grated nutmeg, with its pungently warm and spicy flavor, tastes markedly different from its ground counterpart. If you haven't already tried it, I urge you to do so. It simply makes magic with myriad vegetables (try it with fresh spinach), soups, stews, meats ... you name it. Whole nutmegs in bottles are available in the supermarket spice section. Special nutmeg graters and grinders (many reasonably priced and available in kitchenware shops and gourmet sections of department stores) make quick work out of pulverizing whole nutmegs. You can grate or grind as much nutmeg as you need, then return the "nut" to its bottle for storage. Store whole nutmegs tightly sealed in a cool, dark place for up to 8 months.

Meat and Potato Loaf

I think one of the reasons meat loaf is so popular is because it's malleable—literally and figuratively. For example, you can substitute parsley, basil or spinach for the watercress, green bell pepper for the red pepper, potato chips for the tortilla chips or another type of cheese for the cheddar. If you make this mixture the day before, and refrigerate it so the flavors can blend and mellow, add 10 to 15 minutes to the baking time to allow for the chill factor.

Serves 8

1/2 pound thick-sliced lean smoked bacon

3 tablespoons reserved bacon drippings or olive oil

1 small onion, finely chopped

1 pound russet potatoes, peeling optional, cut into 1-inch chunks

2 medium cloves garlic, minced

2 pounds ground sirloin or chuck (or 1 pound each ground pork or lamb and ground sirloin)

1 1/2–2 packed cups watercress, finely chopped

1/2 cup finely chopped red bell pepper

1 cup shredded cheddar cheese (4 ounces)

1/3 cup beef broth

1 egg, lightly beaten

1/2 teaspoon freshly grated nutmeg

1/2 teaspoon freshly ground black pepper

1/2 teaspoon salt

1 cup crushed tortilla chips, divided

About 1/3 cup barbecue or tomato sauce

Preheat oven to 375°F. Lightly oil a 9 × 13-inch baking pan; set aside. In a large skillet over medium heat, cook bacon until very crisp. Drain bacon on paper towels; crumble when cool. Pour off all but 3 tablespoons bacon drippings. Over medium heat, sauté onion and potatoes in drippings (or olive oil) until onion is nicely browned. Add garlic; cook for 2 minutes. Remove from heat; cool to room temperature.

In a large bowl, combine potato mixture, crumbled bacon, ground meat, watercress, bell pepper, cheese, broth, egg, nutmeg, pepper, salt and $\frac{1}{2}$ cup crushed chips. Mix thoroughly, making sure ingredients and seasonings are thoroughly combined. Turn mixture into prepared pan; form into an oval-shaped loaf about $2\frac{1}{2}$ inches high. Brush exterior of loaf with barbecue or tomato sauce; sprinkle evenly with remaining $\frac{1}{2}$ cup crushed tortilla chips, using a spoon to press chips lightly into surface of loaf. Bake $1\frac{1}{4}$ hours. Let stand 10 minutes before serving.

Meat Loaf Tips

■ Keep your hands clean while mixing a meat loaf mixture by sealing the ingredients in a large, zip-closure plastic bag, then squishing the contents together.

■ Make a meat loaf mixture the day before. Cover and refrigerate to allow the flavors to develop fully.

■ Make two meals in one by doubling a meat loaf recipe and freezing one after baking and cooling. Freeze for up to 6 months.

■ Meat loaf won't stick and cleanup will be quicker if you spray the pan with non-stick vegetable spray or coat it lightly with vegetable oil.

■ For individual meat loaves, bake in greased mini-loaf pans or large muffin tins. Remember that small meat loaves bake faster than large ones.

■ After spooning the meat loaf mixture into the pan, use the back of a spoon to lightly press the mixture down and level the surface.

■ When done, a meat loaf should register about 170°F on a meat thermometer.

■ Let a baked meat loaf stand in the pan for 10 minutes so it can "set," which will make it easier to cut.

■ Leftover meat loaf is great crumbled and added to chilis, soups, or sauces to be served over rice or noodles.

Potato Lasagne

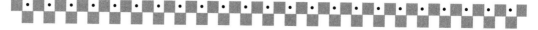

Instead of the traditional noodles, this hearty lasagne employs thin potato slices (cut lengthwise) layered with two fillings—a tomato-sausage béchamel and a basil-ricotta mixture. If you have a food processor with a large feed tube, save time by using small potatoes that will fit lengthwise, and use the 3mm blade to slice the potatoes.

Serves 8

4 ounces shredded mozzarella cheese

4 ounces shredded fontina cheese

3 ounces grated Asiago cheese

4 medium cloves garlic, minced, divided

3 cups packed basil leaves

1 (15-ounce) container ricotta cheese

1/4 cup sour cream

1/4 teaspoon freshly grated nutmeg

1/8–1/4 teaspoon cayenne pepper

Salt

3/4 pound Italian sausage (mild, hot or half of each)

4 tablespoons sausage drippings or olive oil

1 medium onion, chopped

3 tablespoons all-purpose flour

1 tablespoon finely chopped fresh oregano or 1 teaspoon dried

2 tablespoons tomato paste

2 (14 1/2-ounce) cans chopped tomatoes and their juice

3/4 cup milk or half-and-half

Freshly ground black pepper

2 pounds russet or all-purpose potatoes, cut lengthwise into 1/8-inch-thick slices

Preheat oven to 350°F. Lightly oil a 9 × 13-inch baking dish or pan; set aside. In a medium bowl, combine cheeses; set aside. In a food processor fitted with the metal blade, combine 1 minced clove garlic and basil leaves. Process until basil is very finely chopped, stopping machine and scraping down sides of bowl as necessary. Add ricotta, sour cream, nutmeg and cayenne; process until thoroughly combined. Salt to taste; set aside.

Squeeze sausage out of casings into a large skillet. Cook over medium-high heat, finely crumbling as it cooks, until sausage is brown and crispy. Use a slotted spoon to transfer sausage to paper towels to drain. Pour all but 1 tablespoon sausage drippings into a small bowl; set aside. Over medium-high heat, sauté onion, stirring often, until nicely browned. Stir in remaining 3 tablespoons drippings or oil,

remaining 3 minced cloves garlic, flour and oregano; cook 2 minutes, stirring often. Reduce heat to medium. Slowly add tomato paste and tomatoes and their juice, stirring until combined. Add milk or half-and-half; cook, stirring constantly, for 5 minutes. Remove from heat. Stir in sausage; salt and pepper to taste.

Arrange one third of the potato slices in a single layer over bottom of prepared pan, slightly overlapping at the ends and along the sides and filling in any spaces with small potato pieces; top with tomato-sausage béchamel. Repeat with a second layer using one third of the potatoes; spread with ricotta-basil mixture. Repeat final layer with remaining potatoes; sprinkle with cheese mixture. Bake about 1 hour, or until potatoes are tender. Serve hot.

Southern-Style Greens and Potatoes

Although greens have long been popular in the American South, it wasn't until relatively recently that most of the rest of America discovered the full-flavored wonders of collards, kale and chard. Collard greens and kale are both members of the cabbage family, while chard is related to the beet. It's important to remove the tough stems and center ribs of most of these greens. If you're loath to toss them out, boil the stems in water to cover for 20 minutes to extract the flavor. Strain out the solids and freeze the resulting liquid to be used later to lend a husky flavor to soup.

Serves 6

8 slices thick-cut lean smoked bacon

3 tablespoons reserved bacon drippings or olive oil

1 cup fresh bread crumbs

1 small onion, coarsely chopped

2 medium cloves garlic, minced

1 pound collard greens, chard or kale, stems and center ribs removed, leaves coarsely chopped

2 pounds round red or white potatoes, scrubbed and cut into 1/2-inch dice

2 cups hot vegetable or chicken broth

2 tablespoons red wine vinegar

1 teaspoon red pepper sauce

1/2 teaspoon ground allspice

Salt and freshly ground black pepper

Stovetop method: In a large skillet (ovenproof if using the oven method here) over medium heat, cook bacon until very crisp. Drain bacon on paper towels; crumble when cool. Pour off all but 1 tablespoon bacon drippings, reserving remaining fat if using. Sauté bread crumbs over medium-high heat until crisp and well browned. Transfer to paper towels to cool. Heat 2 tablespoons reserved bacon drippings or olive oil in skillet over medium-high heat. Sauté onion, stirring often, until nicely browned. Add garlic and greens; cook 5 minutes, stirring occasionally. Stir in potatoes, broth, vinegar, red pepper sauce, allspice, and salt and pepper to taste; bring to a boil.* Cover and cook over medium heat, stirring occasionally, for about 10 minutes. Remove cover; cook an additional 10 to 15 minutes, or until potatoes are tender and liquid has evaporated. Turn into serving dish; sprinkle top with bread crumbs and crumbled bacon. Serve hot.

Oven method: Follow recipe up to asterisk (*). Sprinkle top with bread crumbs and bacon. Bake, uncovered, in a preheated 400°F oven for about 25 minutes, or until liquid has evaporated and potatoes are tender.

Using nonstick skillets for sautéing or frying means you can decrease by half the oil needed in most recipes.

Mashed Hammy-Yammy Cakes

Yes, it's true, what are sold as yams in the United States are really dark-fleshed sweet potatoes (see page 53), but the title of this recipe appealed to the kid in me. Light-fleshed sweet potatoes may be substituted, but their texture is drier so reduce the bread crumbs to about ¼ cup. These flavorful pancakes are almost fat-free because they're broiled instead of fried. Leftovers make great hash.

Serves 4

1 pound dark-fleshed sweet potatoes

¹/₂ teaspoon ground ginger

¹/₄ teaspoon ground cumin

¹/₄ teaspoon ground coriander

¹/₄ teaspoon ground cinnamon

¹/₈ teaspoon ground cloves

¹/₈ teaspoon cayenne pepper

1 egg yolk, lightly beaten

¹/₂ cup fresh bread crumbs

3 tablespoons finely chopped scallions
(green portion only) or chives

1 (¹/₄-pound) smoked ham slice, shredded
or minced

Salt

Cut unpeeled potatoes in half lengthwise, then crosswise into 1-inch chunks. Cook in boiling water to cover until tender when pierced with the tip of a knife, 10 to 15 minutes; drain immediately. Spear hot potato chunks with a fork and use your fingers to pull off peels; turn peeled potatoes into a large bowl. Using a fork, coarsely mash hot potatoes. Add ginger, cumin, coriander, cinnamon, cloves and cayenne; stir to combine. Add egg yolk, scallions and ham, blending until well combined. Salt to taste. Mixture may be covered and refrigerated overnight at this point.

Position broiler rack 3 inches from heat source. If broiling unit is electric, preheat for 5 minutes. Spray a large baking sheet with nonstick vegetable spray. Use a $1/4$-cup measure to scoop up potato mixture, turning out onto prepared baking sheet. Slightly flatten mound to about 3 inches in diameter. Repeat with remaining potato mixture; cakes should be set at least $1/2$ inch apart. Lightly spray tops of cakes with nonstick vegetable spray. Broil until nicely browned on one side, 5 to 7 minutes. Flip cakes and brown other side. Serve hot.

Winning—How Sweet It Is!

Sweet potatoes were the hands-down nutritional winners in a study conducted by The Nutrition Action Health Letter, in which fifty-eight vegetables were ranked according to their nutritional value, based on the total percentages of U.S. Recommended Daily Allowances of vitamins A and C, folate, iron, copper and calcium. The nearest contender was the carrot, which ranked almost 150 points lower.

Index

Instant-read thermometers, 22

Kale, in southern-style greens
    and potatoes, 104–105
Katahdin potatoes, 52
Kennebec potatoes, 52

Labeling, of meat, 5
lamb:
    buying, 8, 11
    chops with minted onion
        marmalade, French,
        48–49
    cuts of, 10
    Greek osso buco, 95–96
    skewers, Moroccan, 46–47
LaRouge potatoes, 52
lasagne, potato, 102–103
leeks, 62
    -creamy blue-potato bisque,
        63
leftover:
    meat, 7
    meat loaf, 101
    potatoes, 79, 85
lighter fluid, 19
liquor, for cooking, 43
loin, lamb, 11
long white potatoes, 52

Mango gingered pork loin,
    40–41
marbling, 8
marinade, as meat tenderizer, 18
marmalade, minted onion,
    French lamb chops with,
    48–49
mashed hammy-yammy cakes,
    106–107

mashed potato(es), 84–85
    mix-ins, 82–83
    potato varieties for, 57
    with skins, 59
    -stuffed peppers, 90
meat:
    braising, 17
    broiling, 17, 19
    buying of, 5–14
    cooking temperatures, 15–16,
        22
    cuts of, 5, 7–8, 9, 10, 12, 14
    cutting, 11
    defrosting, 7
    doneness, 13, 15, 22
    freezing, 7, 11
    grilling, 19–20
    ground, tips, 36
    hotline, 25
    leftover, 7
    microwaving, 20–21, 23
    panbroiling, 23
    and potato loaf, 100–101
    refrigeration of, 7
    roasting, 23–24
    sautéing, 24
    serving sizes for, 6
    slicing, 11
    stewing, 25
    stir-frying, 25
    storage of, 7
    tenderizing, 18
    see also beef; lamb; pork;
        veal
meatball(s):
    memorable, 35
    muffuletta, 37
    tips for, 36
meat loaf tips, 101
microwave cooking, 20–21,
    23
milk-fed veal, 13
minerals:
    in meat, 6
    in potatoes, 55
    in sweet potatoes, 107

mint(ed):
    carrot toss, 47
    Greek osso buco, 96–97
    onion marmalade, French
        lamb chops with, 48–49
    pesto roasted potatoes,
        76–77
    skordalia, 60–61
mix-ins, mashed potato, 82–83
monosodium glutamate (MSG),
    18
Moroccan lamb skewers,
    46–47
muffuletta, meatball, 37
mushrooms, in mashed
    potatoes, 83
mutton, 8

New potatoes, 52
nutmeg, 99
nutrients:
    in meat, 6
    in potatoes, 55
    in sweet potatoes, 107
nuts:
    ginger-peanut satay, 28–29
    nutty veal niçoise, 34
    skordalia, 60–61
    toasting of, 61

Oil, frying with, 105
olive(s):
    mashed potatoes, 83
    nutty veal niçoise, 34
    salad, Dickie Brennan's,
        38–39
onion:
    mashed potatoes, 83
    minted marmalade, French
        lamb chops with, 48–49
    osso buco, Greek 95–96
oven braising, 17

Index